D1636359

EDD BYRNES

"Kookie" NO MORE

EDD BYRNES

"Kookie" NO MORE

Edd Byrnes

WITH MARSHALL TERRILL

BARRICADE BOOKS INC.

New York

To my son Logan.
"Ah-ha, ah-ha, ah-ha-ha-ha. Daddy . . . Hanky!"

E. B.

To Susan Crawford: A literary agent sent from heaven. This project would have never gotten off the ground without Susan's patience, wisdom, and guidance. Words cannnot express my gratitude for your belief in me. Thanks a million!

M. T.

Published by Barricade Books Inc.
150 Fifth Avenue, New York, NY 10011

Printed in the United States of America.

Library of Congress Cataloging-in-Publication Data
Byrnes, Edd, 1933–
Edd Byrnes : "Kookie" no more / [edited] by Marshall Terrill.
p. cm.
Includes index.
ISBN 1-56980-092-8
1. Byrnes, Edd, 1993– . 2. Actors—United States—Biography.
I. Terrill, Marshall. II. Title.
PN2287.B96A3 1996
791.43'028'092—dc20
[B] 96-27919
CIP

First Printing

TABLE OF CONTENTS

ACKNOWLEDGMENTS

THANKS TO the following: Bill Hux, my personal friend and manager; Roy Hartry for encouraging me not to blow the deal; Dan Barmish for "whatever"; Kevin Boyle for his constant encouragement; Ed Lynch for bringing laughter back into my life again when times were grim; Richard Safran who really should have been cast as Vince Fontaine in *Grease*; Susan Crawford of the Crawford Literary Agency, whose deep belief in this book kept my dream alive to help others. And to Marshall Terrill, who kept probing and probing. At times I felt like I was in a dentist's chair getting my teeth drilled without any anesthetic. Thanks for making our vision come true!

E. B.

MY THANKS must first and foremost go to my parents, Mike and Carolyn Terrill, who have been keeping my dream alive for years—to write books! To Edd Byrnes for his honesty and the opportunity to tell his story. Thanks also goes to author David Morrell, whose belief in my talent and constant encouragement kept me writing when the bad times came along. The same can be said for Charles Champlin, whose generosity astounds me. Thanks to Glen Ammerman for his thoughtful editing. Sandra Stuart for her input and guidance. Lastly, a major thanks goes to Carole and Lyle Stuart for taking a chance with this book when no other publisher had the courage to do so.

M. T.

FOREWORD

OVER THE YEARS, I've had many people ask me why I had not written the story of my life. At first, I didn't think people cared about me that much.

I thought I was too young, but as time went on, many people continued to ask me, "What was it like to be Kookie on *77 Sunset Strip* and to be in all of those movies and traveling all around the world?"

I began to give this matter more and more thought. As I did, I began to realize how terrified I was to write a book about myself. The thought of revealing my entire life, complete with its more sordid moments, scared me to death.

Once I decided to forge ahead with the idea, I promised myself that I would do the job thoroughly and "let it all hang out." I knew that in order to share my life with you, I would have to drop every and all pretenses completely, on every area of my life. This meant putting down on paper my thoughts, feelings, and experiences that I had previously only shared with a small group of close friends.

I agreed to write this book for a variety of reasons: I wanted people to understand that dreams really can come true, despite what others might think. After all, I was a poor kid growing up in a two-bedroom apartment in New York with my mother, brother, sister, and a father who usually was not around. On those rare occasions when he did return, he was invariably drunk and hurling insults.

I would escape to the movies, where I'd feel safe, where I found a sanctuary of warmth and beauty, with the promise of a dream that there was a better life out there. If only I could just believe in this fairy tale.

I drove out to Hollywood to become an actor, like my idols Kirk Douglas, Robert Mitchum, and Burt Lancaster. I landed a series and became an international star. My dream had come true.

The second reason why I took on this endeavor was to give people an insight how Hollywood was back "in those days when."

Lastly, I wanted to write my memoirs because of a need to find an inner peace. I had the notion that if I left myself completely vulnerable, I would somehow gain a better sense of who I was and who I am today. To this end, I have found some peace and serenity.

It's strange to think that after having had worldwide fame, gold records, foreign cars, exotic women, houses in Beverly Hills, apartments in London and Italy, and a host of tangible items, that I would still somehow feel a need to find an inner happiness.

The road I chose brought me great happiness and many things that most people never could hope to have. I feel very fortunate to live the life that I have today. However, the road was not easy. I experimented with drugs and alcohol and the fast lane of Hollywood.

I eventually hit my bottom on August 6, 1982, and ended up in a 12-step recovery program. I've been clean and sober now for more than fourteen years.

To tell you my story is to tell you in detail the life of Eddie Breitenberger, growing up in New York City, with a dream of becoming a star. That dream came true, but not without consequences.

This is my story of the road to an impossible dream finally becoming a reality.

Edd Byrnes
March 1996

"Remember *77 Sunset Strip* on TV? Edd 'Kookie' Byrnes, the parking attendant always combing his hair?

Harry nodded out the window

"They used a place right across the street for exteriors. I used to stand here and watch 'em shoot. Efrem Zimbalist, Jr., and Roger Smith were the stars, but the one you remember is Kookie."

"I wanted blond hair just like his, with the pompadour," Chili said. "I was about ten."

Get Shorty by Elmore Leonard

CHAPTER ONE

Family Secrets

THE YEAR 1960 should have been the greatest time of my life. I had two hit movies under my belt, *Yellowstone Kelly* and *Darby's Rangers.* I was television's first teen idol, known as "Kookie" on *77 Sunset Strip.* The series was an instant smash after its first six weeks, drawing in more than forty million viewers a week. I was told by the head of the Warner Brothers publicity department that I was receiving more fan mail per week than any other actor in the history of the studio. That included Errol Flynn, Humphrey Bogart, and James Cagney when they were at the height of their popularity.

I had a top five record on the *Billboard* charts entitled, "Kookie, Kookie, Lend Me Your Comb," which eventually sold two million copies. Beautiful women were at my beck and call. The money was rolling in, and I was greeted by throngs of screaming fans everywhere I went. I palled around with the likes of Frank Sinatra, Elvis Presley, Kirk Douglas, Robert Mitchum, Burt Lancaster, Bob Hope, William Holden, Michael Caine, Natalie Wood, Robert Wagner,

Sammy Davis, Jr., and a host of other entertainment stars. I was famous not only in the United States but in England, Japan, Spain, Germany, and Italy. Only Elvis Presley could rival my popularity at that time. I had everything a healthy, virile twenty-seven-year-old male could want. The world was definitely my oyster with a little white wine and cracked crab on the side.

During my reign as television's first teen idol, I was hooked on a derivative of heroin called Dranalfa. It contained not just heroin, but an amphetamine as well. In an attempt to get me to open up about my past, my swank Beverly Hills therapist injected me with this strange but potent liquid, which soon loosened my tongue and got me to reveal a nasty secret that I had been carrying around inside of me for years.

A secret so devastating that it could have leveled my career with only a whisper. A secret that I kept painfully hidden from the world for forty-five years.

That is, until now.

* * * * *

I don't remember very much about my father. I have either blocked out his memory because of the anguish I endured as a child, or I just plain don't remember. He was away for most of my childhood in the Army-Air Corps during World War II. To the best of my knowledge, he was a crewman on a B-17 bomber in the Pacific.

My father, Augustus Breitenberger, came from a well-to-do family in the Bronx. His father was a very successful civil engineer who helped design the New York City subway system. Grandfather owned a home on Fort Independence Street and a summer home outside of Plymouth, New Hampshire. He purchased a new Oldsmobile every year, for this was his little reward to himself for all of his hard work.

My father's brother, Paul, was a successful doctor, and his two sisters, Joan and Rita, both married wealthy men. My father was the family's black sheep, and I'm sure this contributed to his life of alcoholism. It seemed as though he always felt less than worthy in their presence.

When we visited his parents in the Bronx, we took the trolleycar. My father never had enough money to buy a car. Maybe that's why I've owned more than thirty-two automobiles in my lifetime. That time without a car left a mark. There was a bar close to the stop before my grandparents' place. My father would leave us sitting on the bench outside while he went inside and proceeded to get fortified. It was only when he came out with a "buzz" that he could deal with his parents.

I don't know how my parents met, but my mother, Mary Byrne, was eighteen when I was born. She was of Irish descent and named me after her father, Edward Byrne, a New York City fireman. Thus I became Edward Byrne Breitenberger.

My father never had what could be called a "professional career." When he was in the service, he achieved the rank of sergeant but was quickly demoted to corporal. I'm almost positive it had to do with his drinking.

What stands out most from my childhood was all the yelling and screaming in our household. Most of this turmoil came from my father's lips. He was not around for a good portion of my earliest years. He left when I was seven and returned when I was twelve. My mother, brother Vincent, and I were living in a two-bedroom apartment in Manhattan on Seventy-eighth Street between Second and Third Avenues. We shared a bathroom with another family and took baths in a tub that was also used to wash clothes. It was a working-class neighborhood, but I didn't know any different. I was not happy to see my father when he returned from the army. I don't have any recollection of him before the age of seven, but I must have known deep in my subconscious that "here comes trouble."

I didn't really know what to call him. Dad, Pop, or Father? I think I ended up calling him Pop, but what I do remember clearly about him was that the man could never hold down a job. My normal day consisted of going down to the local Beergarden, a German saloon, picking up an empty pail, and fetching his beer for him. The owner was the father of a friend of mine and knew the beer was for my old man. It cost thirty-five cents to fill the pail with his beloved suds.

His normal day consisted of laying around on the couch, drinking, and yelling at anyone who crossed his path. I'm reminded of the old joke when I think of Pop: "There's a family sitting around, and there's an elephant running around the living room, and nobody mentions the elephant." Dysfunctional families would rather keep the secrets swept under the carpet than risk confrontation. My father never hit me, but there was always a lot of verbal abuse. He kept everyone in our family walking on eggshells.

My maternal grandmother, Mary, whom I called "Nana," took care of Vincent and me for the most part. Nana's husband had died at an early age in Ireland. She and her four sisters were among the hundred of thousands to flee the Irish potato famine and disembark on Ellis Island, gateway to a new life. Nana lived on the second floor of our building just below us. I used to scrub her kitchen floors on weekends, and she'd pay me for the effort. It was Nana who really raised me. She took me to the local free dentist and made sure I got annual checkups at the doctor's office.

Nana worked at the Pierre Hotel in Manhattan as a chambermaid. She also sold corsets door to door. Everybody, except my father, worked hard to make ends meet.

My father's parents, Augustus and Esther, also took care of us kids during the summer, if I wasn't working to help out my financially strapped parents. My grandparents' two-story home in the Bronx had beautiful gardens in the back filled with fruit trees and flowers. There was even swings for the kids. We also spent a few summers on their lakefront property in Sharon Lake, Connecticut; in Greenwood Lake,

New Jersey; and Lake Winnipesaukee, New Hampshire. Our days revolved around swimming, playing, laughing, and listening to the radio. *The Lone Ranger, The Green Hornet*, and the *Arthur Godfrey Show* were my favorites. Life with my grandparents was in stark contrast to our crowded, cockroach-infested life in Manhattan.

My father was not the only Breitenberger with a drinking problem. Even as a kid, I remember Esther hiding her booze to keep from worrying her husband. She was a "closet alcoholic." I distinctly remember that she'd literally hide her liquor in the closet, and her family would find it. She would be confronted by her husband or one of her daughters, and it would be tense for days afterwards. Years later I realized that my father had probably inherited this dreaded disease called alcoholism.

I also had an Uncle Paddy from Ireland who was the neighborhood drunk, and people used to see him half-sitting, half-balancing on the stoop, with his bottle in a brown paper bag. They were very cruel to him. The disease was on both sides of my family, and it was patiently waiting for my turn in the future.

When my father returned from World War II, he once again got my mother pregnant. I was thirteen when my sister, Jo-Ann, was born. With another mouth to feed, and my father lying on the couch all day not providing any income, I decided that I'd better become the man of the family. I became the breadwinner for the Breitenbergers. In her book, *Daily Affirmations,* Rokelle Lerner writes: "Like many others raised in alcoholic families, I gave up my childhood early. I became serious too soon. I became a caretaker. Old for my years, responsible for adults in my family." That described me. That was *exactly* me.

I'd begin each and every day at 5:30 A.M. selling newspapers. I also worked for a florist and delivered ice to apartments and restaurants. When it snowed, I shoveled sidewalks for the landlord of several buildings to earn some extra money. I'd even skip school to earn a few extra bucks. I tried to stay out on the street as much as possible. I only came home to eat dinner and sleep—that's how much I hated my life at home.

In fact, I skipped so much school that I got held behind in sixth grade because of the emotional toll I was under trying to help out the family finances. My mother whispered to me from the side of her mouth, "We can't tell your father you were left behind because he'll beat the hell out of you." For one whole year, we shared that secret going so far as to hide my schoolbooks with brown-paper covers so that he wouldn't see my true grade level. I felt a lot of shame that I flunked a grade—it implied that I was dumb.

Nevertheless, I continued to work at whatever would earn some money. One day my father caught up with me on Eighty-sixth Street and Second Avenue while I was polishing a man's shoes.

"What the hell are you doing?" an angry voice asked of me from behind.

I turned around, and it was Pop. "I'm working," I eagerly replied. "Ten cents a shine!"

He grabbed me by the collar with one hand, grabbed my box with the other, and took me home. He was very upset. It was rational to him, I suppose, that it was beneath *his* dignity that his son was shining shoes.

It was around this time that I decided I wanted to change my name. Anything not to have the same name as this man who abandoned his wife and children, this man who was an abusive bully, this man who drank, smoked, and couldn't hold down a job because of his drinking. I eventually learned that it is quite common for the children of alcoholics to want to change their name. Someday that wish would come true for me.

When I was thirteen, a neighbor came to me and stated matter-of-factly, "Eddie, your father is down in the cellar dead." I don't really remember what I felt at the time. I do remember the address was 253 East Seventy-eighth Street.

I also remember going down into that dreary basement and seeing his body lying face down over a pile of coals in the furnace room. He also had a sizable bruise on his forehead with dried blood splashed across it.

As I approached his body, there were several people around him. Someone pointed at me and said, "Eddie is his son."

A policeman rifled through his pockets and found twenty-six dollars, which he gave to me.

"I guess this belongs to you now," the man in blue said in a somber tone, careful not to make eye contact with me.

As far as I know, Pop didn't have a checking or savings account, so this was my farewell present from my father. That's all he left the world with, twenty-six dollars.

His death was mysterious. Though I can't prove it, my instincts tell me that there was foul play involved. The janitor in the building was of German descent and spoke very little English. Nonetheless he and my father were always shouting at each other. Call it a gut feeling, but I've always suspected that Pop was murdered by this janitor. When a drunk in New York City was killed in those days, the local police didn't exactly bust their tails investigating the case. Later on, the neighborhood gossip had it that Pop was drunk, hit his head on a large metal pipe, and died of cirrhosis of the liver. I eventually became an alcoholic myself, and I drank a hell of a lot more than my father ever did, and I didn't die of cirrhosis of the liver. Dead in a cellar, lying on top of some coals with a gaping head wound—it is very suspect to me.

Gus Breitenberger was only thirty-six years old when he died. I don't remember attending his funeral.

I had mixed emotions over his death. On the one hand, I was glad he was dead because there would be no more yelling and screaming in our household. I felt this man interrupted our lives and made it very hard to have any kind of family life or serenity. In addition,

I thought of my father as a failure. His death made me strive for success, to know that there was a better kind of life than his.

On the other hand, I was very angry with him because he didn't give me the opportunity to grow up and become eighteen so that I could beat the hell out of him. He denied me the pleasure of revenge when I reached manhood and could give him the proper punishment for all of the years of torture he put our family through.

I became my mother's surrogate husband. I told her, "He can't take care of you anymore, but I can."

Once while my father was away in the war, we had been thrown out of our apartment and our furniture tossed out onto the sidewalk. Neighbors and even my friends made fun of us. I felt incredible shame. My mother couldn't make ends meet, and she couldn't pay the rent. With no place to go and our furniture on the sidewalk, another landlord from across the street took pity on us and put us up in one of his available apartments. I vowed that from that day forward such humiliation would never happen to my family again. I would do anything to avoid being thrown out on the street. Anything!

At fourteen, I began to deliver ice and coal in the freezing mornings that are typical of New York in the winter. I'd meet these guys, Nick and Tony, at the local café before we started our day. Nick, the father, would buy me a doughnut and a cup of coffee. I was stunned the first time he did that. It was the first time someone had ever bought me anything.

Tony would drive the truck while Nick and I delivered ice to homes and restaurants. We'd load up the truck with tongs and cover the ice with big burlap sacks, and sometimes I'd have to lug these blocks of ice up five flights of stairs while Tony read the racing form in the heated cab—not that I minded. I started to develop physically, and it would begin my lifelong obsession with staying in shape.

Tony liked to play the horses, and several days a week, I accompanied him to the track to bet.

Tony was a World War II veteran, and he would entertain me with stories about California, specifically Los Angeles. He made it sound so great that I thought, *one of these days, I have to go there.* The seed was planted.

Tony also passed on a few of his bad habits. He took me to my first burlesque show, in Union City, New Jersey, when I was fifteen. Back in the late forties, the ladies, not quite topless, wore pasties. The show was actually a combination of burlesque and vaudeville. When the dancer went off, a comedian would come onstage and do his schtick for a few minutes. You had to be eighteen to get in, but Tony would buy two tickets and sneak me in. "Stick next to me, kid," he ordered and shuffled me in without fanfare.

When I was fifteen and a half, I decided to drop out of school. I was never what you would call a "dedicated" student. My mind constantly wandered, and I daydreamed a good amount of the time I was there. My favorite subject was geography because I could look at a world map and take these incredible fantasy trips in my head. I meticulously planned where I would go and what I would do when I got there. California always seemed to be at the top of the list.

Another reason why I hated school so much was having to take the bus. The fumes would make me sick to my stomach, so I usually hitched a ride on the back of a trolley car. I also hated the fact that I went to a Catholic school called Saint Jean's on Seventy-sixth Street and Lexington Avenue. The nuns would shout at me and shake their fingers in my face. They would lecture and degrade me, saying, "You're dumb!" or "You're stupid!" It wasn't above these holy people to constantly remind me in front of my classmates that I failed the sixth grade. They humiliated me.

I also wasn't immune to the nuns pinching my cheeks or rapping my knuckles with a ruler. I didn't like kneeling on the hard benches at church or following the strict rules. I especially couldn't stand the taste of communion. The wafers tasted like cardboard, and

I would spit them out in my hand when I thought no one was looking. If the nuns had known better, I imagine they would have been more sensitive to my feelings.

The movies had always been my favorite escape from reality. When I got off work or played hooky, I always took in a flick. I was a regular at the Annex Theater on Seventy-fourth Street between First and Second Avenues. For Saturday morning matinees, I'd pay just fifteen cents to sit on a hard wooden seat and watch three Westerns and a serial. I remember seeing a lot of Charles Starret, Don Red Barry, Lash La Rue, the Three Stooges, and Laurel and Hardy.

The first movie that I can remember was *The Wolfman* with Lon Chaney, Jr., and it scared the hell out of me. But the movies that influenced me most were *The Flame and the Arrow* and *The Crimson Pirate* with Burt Lancaster; *Blood on the Moon* with Robert Mitchum; and especially, *Champion* with Kirk Douglas. There was a scene in the latter movie that I really related to. Kirk Douglas was with Ruth Roman on the beach and his character, Midge Kelly, talked about hiring a detective to track down his father, and then Midge was going to "beat his head off." He went on to say, "Nice guys finish last. I'm going to make some money, take care of the old lady. I'm not going to be a 'Hey you' all my life. I wanna hear people call me 'mister.' I'm going to make something of myself." I walked out of that theater pumped up, thinking, *I really want to become an actor! Champion* was the one movie that I can honestly say changed my life.

At the time, I called these three actors my "three godfathers" because they represented to me what a real man should be. I grew up without much of a father figure, and I looked up to these men as being successful, virile, strong, and compassionate. When I sat inside that dark New York City theater, I would think to myself, *I wish Kirk Douglas, Robert Mitchum, or Burt Lancaster were my father. Then I would be taken care of.* Later when I became an actor, I would develop special friendships with all three men.

I remember going to the Paramount Theater and seeing *His Kind of Woman* with Robert Mitchum and Jane Russell. In those days, the stars would sometimes come out after the movie was over and tell a story or funny anecdote. Once Bob Mitchum actually sang a song. I can still hear him. "Pretty baby. Everyone loves my baby, that's why I'm in love with you." I can still see what he was wearing—a blue blazer, pink shirt, dark blue tie, light gray slacks, and black-and-white shoes.

Burt Lancaster made a special appearance at the Capitol Theater on Broadway for *The Crimson Pirate.* He performed some acrobatics with his costar, Nick Cravat. Those were the days! Can you imagine a movie star doing that today?

The movies gave me hope, inspiration, and something to strive for to get out of the poverty that plagued my family. One time, when I got to know Kirk Douglas, we got into a funny conversation about which one of us had been the poorest. Kirk said to me, "Edd, you think you were poor? Betty Bacall had to give me a overcoat in the wintertime because it was too cold." I responded, "Kirk, you think that was poor? I used to stuff newspapers down my jacket to keep my stomach warm. At least you had an overcoat to keep you warm!"

My poverty got me to thinking about becoming an actor. I didn't really want to be an actor; more specifically, I wanted to be a *movie star.* A movie star is the closest thing in the United States we have to royalty. In order to become a movie star, I had to overcome many obstacles in my life. I was a high-school dropout with a thick New York accent and no experience in the theater whatsoever.

It would take all of my drive and ambition to become a success in acting. Help would come along in many forms, but in exchange for that help, I had to do certain things that I have long kept secret. A secret that I thought I would take to my grave.

CHAPTER TWO

Exposed

GYMNASTICS became a big part of my physical development. At fourteen, I finally discovered something at which I excelled. Henry Schraeder, the gym instructor at the New York Turn-Virien, a German-operated gymnasium on Eighty-fifth Street and Lexington Avenue, encouraged and nurtured my acrobatic skills. I actually became very good at tumbling, parallel bars, high bars, and rings. I brought home more than my fair share of medals.

I usually worked out for two hours, five times a week, after I finished delivering ice. The workout kept me fit, and I took to the sport like a fish to water. I was a natural, and in addition, gymnastics kept me out of trouble.

It was there at the Turn-Virien that I met my first love and girlfriend, Inga Puthe. Inga and I liked to take in Alan Ladd movies and dated heavily. The first time we tried having sex, I didn't know what to do. I was so inexperienced, I just fumbled around in the dark. We never did have actual intercourse.

I was really head over heels in love with Inga. We were officially going steady for some time, when one day out of the blue, she told me that she could no longer see me.

"Why?" I asked, holding back my tears.

"I'm seeing Tommy Wonder."

Tommy Wonder was a professional dancer who had his own revue at Radio City Music Hall and was "an older man" at the ripe old age of twenty-one. He also made good money and could afford to take Inga out to expensive restaurants and first-run movies. I couldn't offer Inga those things, but I still objected to her new love-interest.

"He has his own show at Radio City Music Hall. What can you offer me?" she asked rather crassly.

In my fury, I spouted out, "I'll show you, Inga! I'll become a lot more famous than Tommy Wonder, and you'll be crawling back to me. You just wait and see," I said, shaking my fist at her. My first love broke my heart into little pieces.

I had my first sexual encounter with a female when I was sixteen and working in a machine shop. One of my coworkers asked me if I'd like to go with him to Spanish Harlem to a house of prostitution.

"It'll cost you five bucks to get laid," he informed me.

He took me to this woman, I gave her the five dollars, and she lifted her skirt for me. It was the worst sexual experience of my life. It was very cold and unemotional. I was very disappointed. I thought, *Is this what it's like? What's the big deal?*

I drove a 1937 Ford (it cost me $125) every day across the Fifty-ninth Street Bridge to get to Queens where I was a drill-press operator and earned all of eighty-five cents an hour. The machine shop had produced ammunition for our side in World War II. The owner of the place, ironically, was German, and he was very good to me.

The foreman, Leo, was a little man who used to give me all sorts of odd jobs around the shop. I was a hard worker who would rather keep busy than do nothing. One day I was on his heels, asking him what task I could take on next. Leo shouted, "Eddie, stop following me around like a puppy dog!" It really hurt my feelings. I was sensitive to any kind of criticism from a man.

I also had a coworker who was Jewish, and he always called me a "schmuck." I didn't know what the word meant until I asked somebody at the shop. After I was told it meant "prick," I confronted him. We had a few words and fortunately we didn't have to duke it out, but he never called me a schmuck again.

The shop always had these movie magazines lying around with stories on Hollywood and the stars. For fifteen minutes in the morning and fifteen minutes in the afternoon, I'd take these magazines in the bathroom stall and read them from cover to cover. I fantasized about having this wonderful life away from New York City, going to Hollywood, becoming a movie star. I wanted everything those magazines glamorized: the beautiful girls on my arm, tuxedos, the luxurious homes, and lounging around poolside complete with champagne. That vision also included fine automobiles and attending world premieres with the paparazzi snapping away, flashbulbs popping. It was all a fantasy, but it was a fantasy that would eventually get me out of the pits of the concrete jungle that I called home.

There never seemed to be enough money to pay off all our expenses. Even with my regular job at the machine shop, it wasn't enough to cover the rent. My mother worked in a defense plant, which was nothing more than a sweatshop. There were four hungry mouths to feed and there was always the rent, gas, or some other bill overdue. That's why it began.

"Hustling" is not a world that one aspires to; it is a world one just happens to fall into. New York City is not Ames, Iowa. In the Big Apple, there's only one law, and it is survival of the fittest. It still goes on today, and I'm sure it will continue long after I leave this earth.

I was drawn into the world of hustling when I began posing at the age of seventeen for magazine covers. Once I made the cover of *Inside Detective*, the modeling jobs became more frequent.

Because of my bodybuilding, and gymnastics, I had a pretty good physique. I wasn't a bad-looking kid, either.

At the gym, I became friendly with a group of guys who were also into bodybuilding. We were approached by a famous photographer named Lon Hannigan. Lon was gay and grossly overweight, but he was a jovial and very generous man.

Lon loved beautiful young boys and would invite us to his nicely decorated midtown Manhattan studio. There he would offer to take photos of us for free to get our modeling careers off and running. Not nude photos mind you, but "skimpy." We usually posed in a tiger-skin loincloth with Jerome Kern playing in the background. Lon loved Jerome Kern's music.

At the time, Lon was living with a young bodybuilder named Raul. We had nothing sexual to do with Lon at the time, but once he asked that we urinate on him while he masturbated sitting in the bathtub. At first, we laughed at his request because we thought he was joking. He insisted, and we fulfilled his request. We obliged him because he took photos of us for free, took us to the theater and movies, and whenever we'd visit his apartment, he'd cook us these incredible meals. In return for his generosity, we felt considerably indebted to him.

Knowing we were hurting for cash, Lon asked us, "Look, how would you like to make a $100?" A hundred dollars in those days was a fortune to us, and then he proceeded to tell us about what he had in mind knowing that he had piqued our interest.

For my first hustling assignment, I was asked to do some nude posing while an older gentleman acted like he was sketching me for an art class. He asked to fondle me, but I told him no. I later learned he was a Rothschild from the famous Rothschild family of New York. He had a beautiful apartment on Sutton Place overlooking the East River. He had this weird quirk. Strangely, he liked to serve me a glass of milk with 7-Up.

Lon eventually became our pimp, and his sole purpose was to set us up on dates with older, rich men. One of my dates was a man called Mr. Henry. He was a mysterious guy, but I believe he was a major executive for one of the television networks. Mr. Henry came to Lon's place to meet with me, and we undressed and got into bed. I was very passive. Afterward, he gave me the hundred-dollar bill and he was gone. I only saw him once.

Another one of my dates was Walter Chrysler of the Chrysler automobile family. Lon and the group of young bodybuilders visited Mr. Chrysler's plush townhouse on the east side of Manhattan for a dinner party. After dessert, Walter invited us down to his wine cellar which he had converted into a torture chamber. Walter's particular fetish was that he was into being burned. He asked each of us take a lit cigarette and put it out on a part of his flesh. He'd sigh when the cigarette made contact with his skin. I personally could not fulfill this strange and kinky request, and I had to kindly bow out. It was disgusting.

It was a strange world I had been introduced to: art, wealth, sadism, limousines, sex for money, theater, and fine restaurants.

This lifestyle was also downright dangerous. I never knew what would greet me behind the door when one of my dates opened it. Even though Lon had set up the dates, there was always an air of uncertainty and danger.

As you will discover, I am very much a heterosexual man who loves and adores the company of women. Although my hustling phase was strictly for money, I discovered later through intense therapy that I was also searching for something I had never received—the love of a man, the love my father had never given me.

My life changed completely when I was introduced to John F. Harjes. I met John through a Russian art dealer.

"Eddie, I vant chu to meet a very nice man. Very vealthy man."

For our first date, we agreed to meet for lunch at the Oak Room in the Plaza Hotel. He was instantly attracted to me.

What I remember most about John is that he was always impeccably dressed. He usually wore a coat and tie with a burgundy carnation in his lapel.

John was beyond generous, and I actually became quite fond of him after awhile. Not in a sexual way, but he eventually became my mentor and teacher.

I found out that John's father was J. P. Morgan's partner in the banking business. To this day, the Morgans have a bank in New York.

He soon showered me with presents the way a woman would be showered with gifts. I was an impressionable seventeen-year-old, and I was in awe of his considerable wealth. John bought me fine tailor-made suits, ties, and sports jackets from Dunhill's Tailor; watches and identification bracelets from Cartier; Italian loafers and cuff links adorned with sapphires, rubies, and gold.

John also rented a nice garden apartment for me on Seventy-second Street between Lexington and Park Avenues. He wanted a garden apartment so that he could take his dogs out for walks. He always had a dog with him.

John also opened a checking account for me, in which he deposited three thousand dollars. He said, "Eddie, I want you to be able to write a check for your mother's rent when she needs it, and also, I want you to have some walking-around money." He made sure that my family was well taken care of. John had cattle on his property near Blairstown, New Jersey, and walk-in freezers with meat hanging all over the place. Every time I visited, he encouraged me to take home twenty pounds of steak. He'd have his butcher chop it up and wrap it, and I'd bring home these huge cuts of beef to my family. Despite the fact that it was repulsive going to bed with this man, he was very kind.

We enjoyed a Pygmalion-type relationship. John was the teacher, and I was his prized pupil. John had been educated in the finest schools in Switzerland, spoke several languages fluently, and took pleasure in passing on his fine tastes and invaluable wisdom to me.

He showed me the sights in Paris and informed me of the importance of everything I was experiencing. He also took me to Los Angeles for the first time in my life. He asked, "Eddie, where would you like to visit?"

"I've always wanted to see Hollywood."

We flew first class to Los Angeles and took a taxi to the Beverly Hills Hotel where we stayed together in a bungalow. The hotel was then the best place in town. I took one look around the gardens and said to myself, *I've arrived in Paradise. I've definitely got to come back here.*

After we settled in, John asked me, "As long as we're here, why don't I buy you a car, and we'll drive back to New York. What kind of car do you want?"

Stunned, I said, "I don't know. What about a Cadillac convertible?"

The next thing I knew, we were in a Cadillac dealership on Wilshire Boulevard. John paid cash for the car on the spot. He put the car in my name, and we drove around Beverly Hills shopping till we dropped and playing for a whole week. We drove back to New York (with a brief stop in Las Vegas) with the top down.

When I got back to my mother's apartment, nineteen years old, pulling up in a Cadillac convertible, all of the neighbors were asking, "What the hell is going on?" But my mother didn't ask, and I wasn't volunteering any information. She must have known what was going on, but by then my father had been dead for five years, and I was the head of the family. What could she say?

John was bisexual and was married at the time to his second wife, who was also very wealthy. Surprisingly, John did like women. He was good friends with heiress and designer Gloria Vanderbilt and socialite Frances Carpenter. I even witnessed John having sex with a few women at a nude swimming party at his farm in New Jersey.

John's second marriage eventually fell apart. It seems that his wife was having an affair with one of the farmhands, a fellow named Vernon. When John found out, he threw her out of the house. She ended up marrying Vernon.

Once I met John, I put all dating behind me, except for women. I brought them over frequently to the apartment John rented for me. He furnished the place with some valuable art and expensive antique furniture.

John employed a maid and laundress named Gertrude who worked for him primarily at Blue Crest, the farm in Jersey. She reported directly to him. Gertrude was like a Nazi commandant. "Zere vere bobby pins und panties in Edd's bed ven I vas cleaning up, Mistah Harjes," she'd tell him with a thick German accent. John would then ask me, "Are you screwing all of these girls in my apartment?" I'd have to soothe John. "I threw a little party at the apartment last night. It was no big deal, believe me." That apartment saw more than its fair share of models, dancers, show girls, and actresses. I especially loved dancers and discovered they were very sexual and expressive by nature. I always had girlfriends on the side while I was with John.

It gave John real pleasure to educate me on the finer things in life. He loved taking me to museums, art galleries, and plays. I think his love of the theater rubbed off on me, because it was then that I really started to think seriously about acting as a possible future.

We saw *Picnic* with Ralph Meeker playing Hal Carter, my favorite part of all time. Paul Newman was also in the play as Alan Seymour and was Ralph's understudy. I met Ralph from drinking in the theater bar. He'd always have a few drinks after the show, and I'd see him hanging out with Joe Hardy, Clifton James, and Martin Landau. Years later, I would tour with that play in the Hal Carter role. Also during that time on Broadway, we saw a young James Dean in *See the Jaguar.*

Once Lon Hannigan had taken me to see the play *I've Got Sixpence,* starring Edmund O'Brien. Lon said, "Let's go backstage and meet Edmund O'Brien." I asked, "You're kidding me, Lon?"

I'll never forget seeing Mr. O'Brien taking off his makeup in his dressing room and Lon introducing me to him. "Eddie wants to be an actor," Lon announced. The actor looked at me like I was nuts and offered no words of encouragement. I handed over my *Playbill* so he could sign it. I reminded him of that incident when we did a movie together a few years later. It turns out he had given me that strange look back in the dressing room because of his poor eyesight. He was trying to focus so he could see me. Mr. O'Brien was an incredible actor and won an Academy Award for his performance in *The Barefoot Contessa.*

Kirk Douglas's performance in *Detective Story* also had a profound impact on me. I must have seen it ten times when it was first released.

Once I told John Harjes that I wanted to become an actor, he encouraged me wholeheartedly. He couldn't have been more pleased. He even shelled out twelve hundred dollars for me to get the best plastic surgeon in New York City to straighten my nose. I didn't want my father's last name, and I certainly didn't want my mother's nose with which I was born. So I changed them both. I guess in retrospect I was trying to create a new identity. I wanted to be a new person, and acting was the perfect occupation into which to escape.

I never went to an acting school or studied under a famous New York teacher. Though they were available to me, I was too shy to get up in front of a class and perform, so I would just sit in and watch from the sidelines. I didn't know that in acting I had to learn a craft and memorize lines. It was more of a fantasy for me. It was all Errol Flynn, Burt Lancaster, and fencing and acrobatics. I didn't know that training was part of the program. My concept of acting took a more dramatic form in what I would term *reality.*

When I was eighteen, I made friends with a guy in my neighborhood gym named Joe Finn. Joe was only one year older than I, but much more streetwise.

He was a good-looking, beefier version of Tony Curtis. Joe stood five feet nine inches and was built like a bull. We had a mutual interest in acting and became friends right away. Although he was already married and had a couple of kids, Joe always managed to have time for me.

Joe also got me a job with *Time/Life* as a driver. I even got my chauffeur's license. The job didn't last long though. During my lunch hour, I was doing push-ups between two desks and was told that my services were no longer needed. My actions were interpreted as "goofing off."

Joe Finn pumped a lot of iron and beat up a lot of guys. The man had no fear and had a lot of anger in him. He would beat the shit out of anyone who looked at him cross-eyed. Luckily for me, Joe genuinely liked me.

With a wife and two kids, Joe realized that he couldn't become an actor, so he decided to become a cop. He therefore encouraged me to put my heart and soul into acting.

"You're young and single. You wanna learn about actin'? Come with me," he said confidently.

Joe was promoted to detective after only one year on the police force. He made that many arrests.

Detective Finn was absolutely fearless, but one time we went into Harlem to make a drug bust in this old dilapidated building. It was at night, and Joe had been tipped off that this guy was a major drug dealer. Joe knocked on the door, and when no one answered, he kicked it in. The room was pitch black, and we couldn't see anything until he turned on the light. What we saw will horrify me to my dying day: wall-to-wall cockroaches. Millions of them all over the place. They covered every square inch of this apartment, and this guy who lived there was so stoned out of his mind, they were crawling all over him, including his face, and he just stared into space. Even Joe didn't want the "collar" that bad, and we both got the hell out of there faster than you could say Roach Motel.

Joe's plan for my acting career was to take me along on busts and act as his partner in the interrogation room. The "good cop/bad cop" routine. In a reversal of roles, Joe for once got to play the good cop, and I was the bad cop. That was my formal training for acting.

What the police did in those days was to take a telephone book and slam it on the head of the person they were interrogating to get him to talk. It didn't leave any bruises. One good whack over the head usually did the trick.

"What's your name?" I'd ask in a polite manner.

When I got no reply, I pulled out the phone book and let the Yellow Pages do the talking.

WHAP!

"Don't make me have to do that again."

Those phone books, I discovered, had more than one use.

"Hey," replied the criminal, "I was an innocent bystander."

"Don't lie to me, Charlie."

WHAP!

"I'm tellin' ya da truth."

"Charlie, your breakin' my heart."

"It's da truth, I swear."

WHAP!

"But it's da truth. I swear on my mother's grave, I'm innocent."

"Take this bum outta here and lock 'em up." And then Joe would dutifully come over and escort the convict to his cell.

Now with my acting career well underway, or so I thought, I began to look for legitimate work. I met a fellow actor named Edd Kramer, and he began taking me along to his auditions. My very first acting job was on television as an Indian in a skit with Joe E. Brown on *The Buick Circus Hour* for $125. After that, the pickings were slim.

I also did a stint for *Coke Time With Eddie Fisher*. I shook Mr. Fisher's hand and in an instant, a signed eighty-by-ten photo of himself was shoved in my other hand. When I got to know Eddie much better, I ribbed him about this act of vanity.

When I wasn't acting, I was studying others performing their craft. *On the Waterfront* was filmed in Hoboken, New Jersey, and I watched Marlon Brando, Lee J. Cobb, and Karl Malden work during the filming.

In a couple of scenes, I managed to sneak myself into extra shots without the director's knowledge, the great Elia Kazan. I was in the scenes where the dockworkers lined up to go inside a warehouse and where the longshoremen watched a fight between Brando and Cobb. I've tried to find myself in those filmed scenes, but there are so many extras that it's impossible to pick me out.

My goal was to get to Hoboken every day, find out where the company was filming, and watch those great actors work. I saw the scene where Brando and Eva Marie Saint were walking in the playground, Eva Marie Saint dropped her glove, and Marlon picked it up and played with it. It's a famous scene, but the take in the movie was total improvisation. While rehearsing, Eva Marie Saint never dropped her glove. When Kazan yelled action, she accidentally dropped it, and Brando kept going with the scene. He bent down to pick up the glove, caressed it, handed it back to Eva, and left. It was pure genius.

I was in the presence of truly great filmmaking, because even watching it as a spectator, it was the most realistic acting I had ever seen. It was an exhilarating experience.

My ultimate goal was to get to Hollywood, but I knew that I wasn't quite ready. John Harjes introduced me to Leonard Altobel, the producer and director of the Litchfield Summer Playhouse in Litchfield, Connecticut. He said that if I went up for summer stock and became an apprentice, he would cast me in a few of his plays and help me get an Actors' Equity card.

Since I was the only student there with a car, in addition to building sets, Leonard put me to work driving around and nailing up posters. In return, he cast me in ten plays. I nailed posters in the morning, rehearsed during the day, and performed at night.

I started out with small parts and later graduated to feature parts. I can remember doing *Picnic* and *The Caine Mutiny Court Martial.* We performed a play a week for one whole summer. It proved to be excellent training. I gained a lot confidence in myself. If an actor has stage training, it's so much better than starting off in television or in the movies. If an actor can get up on that stage and perform for two straight hours, he or she can do any kind of motion picture work or television roles.

One of the towns that I visited that summer was Plymouth, New Hampshire, where my grandfather had owned a home. I decided to find that old house. I talked to a lot of the storekeepers, and sure enough, they did remember the name Breitenberger. I was also told that the old house was torn down in order to make room for a new highway. I then took a stroll through Plymouth and felt really comfortable walking and taking in some of my past. I had definitely been there before.

When I got back from summer stock, I was introduced to a director who was ready to produce a play in Detroit. He took one look at me and said, "I'm doing *Golden Boy*, and I think you'd be great in it. Why don't you come to Detroit?" That was my audition. I later on found out he was gay, and I had a hard time keeping him at bay.

I had performed in featured parts before, but nothing compared to the experience of the lead role in a play. I was to play Joe Bonopart, the role that made William Holden a star in the film.

To be a leading man was my dream. I quickly discovered that usually the norm in any play was that the leading actor and actress became lovers. It was no exception this time. My leading lady was an older woman, thirty-five to my nineteen, and was quite beautiful. Imagine my pleasant surprise when she walked up to me a week before we opened and discreetly said, "After opening night, I want to make love to you." I was dumbfounded, but managed to reply with a blank stare and a very simple, "OK." Obviously, that made for one very long week. I counted the days, hours, minutes, seconds, and milliseconds until opening night was over and the curtain came down.

After the play, I traded in the Cadillac convertible that John Harjes had bought for me in exchange for an Oldsmobile 88 and eighteen hundred dollars in cash. The time had come for John and me to part ways. I was getting fed up with the whole routine with him and my life as a male prostitute. I was also facing so much rejection in New York City that I felt that I needed a change of luck and scenery. In addition, not many movies were being shot in New York. Hollywood was where my dreams would come true. If I could make it there, I could make it anywhere, but not in New York, New York.

John didn't like the idea of my leaving, but he didn't try to dissuade me. He wished me well, we hugged, and we parted as friends.

In 1955 armed with a car, eighteen hundred dollars in my pocket, and a blinding ambition to succeed, I drove from New York to California to become a movie star.

Like so many flocks of escapists and fellow dreamers, I sought Hollywood in search of a better life.

CHAPTER THREE

Sunny California

I ARRIVED in Los Angeles on September 30, 1955. The reason I remember the date so well is that it was the same day that James Dean crashed his Porsche Spider into a truck and died on a lonely California highway near Fresno. Hollywood was looking for a new teen idol.

The first thing I did was to rent a place to live. All I could find was a furnished room in a private home on Hollywood Boulevard off Sunset Plaza Drive for fifty dollars a month.

On one of my first days in Beverly Hills, I was cruising along in my white Olds 88 with the top down. At a stop sign right beside me was Natalie Wood. She was driving a white 1955 T-Bird. She looked so good in it that I decided to trade my Olds in for a T-Bird. Back then, they were very inexpensive. Natalie would eventually become a dear friend.

I came to California with John Harjes's blessing and in my possession was a letter of introduction from his friend, socialite Frances

Carpenter, addressed to Ross Hunter, a successful film producer at Universal Studios. It was Hunter who produced all of the Rock Hudson and Doris Day movies.

In my naiveté, I thought I'd pop over and see him, give him the letter from Frances, have him sign me to a seven-year contract, and be on my way to stardom. I soon discovered it wasn't done that way.

"How is Frances? So you want to be an actor?" Mr. Hunter asked of me, making polite conversation. When I left the office at Universal, I thought it would only be a matter of time before I became a movie star. He never called. He never even offered to introduce me to casting people. Nothing.

What a prick!

Hollywood in the late fifties was a much kinder place than it is now, but it was still a tough place to crack. I arrived at the tail end of the seven-year contracts that the studios had each actor sign. In order to get one of those coveted contracts, I had to have an agent. That proved to be pretty tough because I was not a member of the Screen Actors Guild.

I began the search for an agent by plastering my eight-by-ten photo and résumé in the offices of agencies, but I even went further than that: I left photos on the windshields of the owners of the agencies. One in particular was Jack Pomeroy of the Jack Pomeroy Agency. Miraculously, he called me and said, "Yeah kid, you've got a good look. Come in and see me."

Pomeroy signed me but never got me any work that I can remember. I don't even know if he tried. The money I brought from New York was dwindling, and I had to find work even if it meant climbing over the fences of studios and sneaking in, which I did.

Old studios like ZIV, Four Star, California, Republic, Warner, and MGM had tight security, but I somehow managed to avoid being caught. I'd walk around the lot looking for producers and directors. This is how I thought one got discovered. Hollywood was a town that had a lot of buffers, and I never got past the secretaries of important executives who had heard and seen it all. I was quickly shown the door many times.

The first job I landed was in the TV series, *Wire Service*, starring George Brent. I had a scene with Mr. Brent where I played the role of a gas station attendant, washing his windshield and having a conversation with him. We were shooting a long shot, and the director yelled, "Cut and print." Then the camera was moved closer to get a closeup of me.

"What are we doing?" I asked naively.

"A closeup," said the director. "We're going to do the scene again, but this time, we're going to give you a closeup."

"What's that?" I asked, I'm sure, giving the director reason to think that I might have been in possession of a room-temperature IQ.

"We're going to splice the master shot and cut it with your closeup in the editing room."

"Oh . . ."

They didn't teach this on the stage in Litchfield, Connecticut. I had a long way to go in this town if I didn't even know what a closeup was.

Finally, after a few weeks, I auditioned for a play called *Tea and Sympathy* and was hired at $22.50 a week for five weeks. Two other unknown actors were in the play with me, a fellow named Jack Nicholson and a fellow named Michael Landon.

Jack and I didn't get too close, but he was a nice enough guy. He had a funny New Jersey accent and was very thin. The thing I remember most about Jack was his shit-eating grin. Jack had a couple of lines in the play, but I never thought that he was that good an actor. Though at the time, I really didn't pay too much attention to his acting. The ironic thing was that stardom was right around the corner for Michael and me, but it was a long, hard climb for Jack to make.

He struggled for more than twelve years before leaving his mark in *Easy Rider*. But when he hit it, he hit it big! He also has turned into a gifted actor to boot.

Mike Landon and I became very good friends and continued our friendship for many years. Michael, it seemed in those early days, always had a new car, a very big house, and, especially for an actor, a lot of money.

He also had these large ears that stuck out. When he worked, he'd have to have them pasted back. Later on, he had an operation to correct the problem.

Mike was married at the time to his first wife, Dody, an older woman, and they had a few kids running around the house. Often I would take a date to his house, and we'd have dinner and watch horror movies. Mike loved horror movies.

I knew that Mike was destined to be a star. In the play, the director would tell him, "In this scene, I want you to cry," and then the director would snap his fingers, and Mike would have tears streaming down his face. He was a very sensitive guy and, at the same time, a very funny man. He loved to laugh.

Eve Miller was the leading lady in *Tea and Sympathy* and again, an older woman with whom I had an affair. Eve eventually achieved success in a few movies, such as *The Big Trees* with Kirk Douglas, but she definitely liked younger men. During the course of the play, she slept with me, Jack, and Mike, no one knew about the others until years later when it came up in a conversation. Eve Miller was a terrific lady with a ferocious sexual appetite.

After *Tea and Sympathy*, I went on a long dry spell before I found any work, and I was running out of money. My friend, Joe Finn, the cop in New York City, agreed to send me $100 a month to sponsor my acting career. Joe by then was on the take and probably siphoned off tens of thousands of dollars in kickbacks. He used to come over to my mother's apartment and ask her to store his brown grocery bags of money in her closet. One day she took a peek and spotted thousands of dollars. She was too petrified of him to even think of taking a dollar for herself. She must have suspected it was "dirty" money.

Even Joe's $100 a month was barely covering my bills. I only had $50 left over for rent, food, a car payment on the '55 T-Bird, and gas for the car. It was just enough to keep my head above water.

One sure way of getting money was the pawnshop that I became familiar with on Vine Street, just half a block south of Hollywood Boulevard. I once received thirty-five dollars for the gold Cartier identification bracelet that John Harjes had bought me, way below the value of that trinket. I'd also hock my sports jackets for five dollars while I got ten dollars for a suit. When I'd get a small role on television, I'd go back to the pawnshop and reclaim all the items. This went on for quite awhile until I got my contract at Warner Brothers that gave me a regular income.

In fact, I was so broke then that every day my girlfriend, Asa Maynor, would cook me a hard-boiled egg and leave it in her mailbox so that I could have something to fill my empty stomach while I made the rounds at the studios.

I first met Asa when I was doing a television show called *Matinee Theater*, starring Dean Stockwell. I went to this audition and noticed two gorgeous eighteen-year-olds, Asa Maynor and June Blair. June later married David Nelson, son of Ozzie and Harriet, and brother of Rick.

Our relationship started off very slowly, which was really different for me. We continued to see each other after the show, and Asa was performing in a play called *Middle of the Night,* in the Kim Novak role. She invited me to the play, and, afterward, I went backstage to congratulate her on a job well done.

I mustered up the courage to ask her out, and she said, "I have a date."

"Break it," I coolly ordered.

She gave me a sidelong glance, but she broke the date.

Sally Kellerman became a mutual friend of ours, and because I was afraid, if not totally petrified of falling in love, I asked Sally to come with us and do things as a threesome. Sally had a big crush on me. She later told me that I was the first love of her life. I never had an affair with Sally, but she developed into a beautiful woman and also happens to be a fine actress. I love her voice. We were in one film together, the forgettable *Reform School Girl,* my first starring role in a movie.

I'd constantly fix up Sally with one of my friends, and we'd often double date. Sally was the butt of many cruel jokes. I guess it was because she was so gullible and would have the greatest reactions to our gags. Once, Asa and I brought her to the home of my friend, Don Vosdick. He had left his apartment door open just a crack, and we all went inside. Don was lying on the floor with fake blood all over these white sheets and himself. Sally went bananas and literally screamed bloody murder. We were always doing something horrible to her, and still, she tagged along on all our dates.

Asa and I got along really well. In fact, too well. She was always fun to be around. She had a very sexy, shapely body. In addition, she had an infectious laugh. It scared me to fall in love at twenty when I had so much in life that I wanted to accomplish. I was in love with her, no question about that, but I put her off and dated other women behind her back. I also made love to a lot of other women during that period, and she'd get angry, but we always managed to get back together.

Finally, I caught a big break when I landed a very capable agent, Jack Donaldson of the Donaldson Agency. Later, I found out that he was gay, and I thought, *What the hell is going on here? I left that life behind me in New York. Is everyone in Hollywood gay, too?* Jack had quite a crush on me. I was uncomfortable being with him because he always wanted to touch me. Mr. Donaldson took me around to the big studios and introduced me to several talent scouts and casting people. One casting agent at Warner Brothers, Solly Buyano, on meeting me told me point blank, "You need to lose that New York accent."

"What are youse talkin' bout?" I responded, quite offended.

"You're not contract material."

Ouch!

About one year later when I was playing the role of Kookie on *77 Sunset Strip* and was the hottest actor in television, I'd see Solly on the lot and would rub his face in the dirt. "Solly, you said I wasn't contract material, and now I'm getting fifteen thousand fan letters a week. I'm the number one star at Warner Brothers." I was ribbing him hard and enjoying my revenge. It was one of the few times he was wrong.

My first feature film was *Fear Strikes Out*, starring Anthony Perkins as the professional baseball player Jimmy Piersall. If you blinked, you missed me. I played one of Tony's teammates.

I had often seen Tony Perkins around town before we ever made the picture. Tony never drove; he hitchhiked everywhere he went. When we were filming together, I'd see him thumbing for a ride on Sunset, so I'd pick him up in my T-Bird and take him to Paramount. He was a nice guy, but very quiet.

I used to watch other actors work even when I wasn't. In *Fear Strikes Out*, Tony's character was a baseball player bullied by his father, played by Karl Malden. In the film's pivotal scene, Malden pushed Tony over the edge. Malden yelled at him, "You've gotta be a better player!" and then Tony totally lost it. He started to shout and scream. He grabbed Karl by the shirt, and banged him up against the wall. The director, Robert Mulligan, yelled, "Cut. That's a print."

I was mesmerized by Tony's performance, and when the scene was over, I went over to congratulate him. "Tony, that was great. Fantastic scene. You were so realistic. What did you get in touch with to make you turn loose like that?"

What he said was unbelievable. "See that script girl over there? She was timing the scene with her watch. She was looking at her watch, then looking at me, then looking down at the script, following me line for line. Then I began to hear her watch ticking and hear her turning the pages. She was following what I was saying—watching her head move from side to side just drove me fucking nuts and I lost it."

I didn't have any dialogue with Karl Malden, but he's known as one of the best actors in the business. I once spoke to Kirk Douglas about his son, Michael, doing the TV series, *The Streets Of San Francisco*.

I asked Kirk, "Did you want Michael to do the series, or did you want him to go right into movies?"

He smiled ruefully, "Oh, no. I wanted Michael to work with Karl Malden every single day and learn from him." When Kirk Douglas says that, you have to be a great actor.

My next film was a B-movie called *Johnny Trouble*. I played a teenaged hood. The film was only memorable for me because during shooting I became good friends with actor Stuart Whitman, and we would later star in a movie called *Darby's Rangers* with James Garner.

An anecdote about Stuart: Warner Brothers signed him to the standard seven-year contract, and they said he could be in *Darby's Rangers* if he agreed to sign the contract. The contract was sent, and for some reason, Stuart never signed it. Stuart was getting $500 a week when he finished the picture. Warner Brothers legal department, not keeping on top of the situation, didn't know that Stuart hadn't signed the new contract. Twentieth Century-Fox made a generous offer of $1,000 a week to the now contract-free actor, and he laughed all the way to the bank. It wasn't often that actors back then got the best of the studios. I would find that out the hard way in the ensuing months.

Life Begins at 17 was made at Columbia and was the last film I made before I went under contract to Warner Brothers. My leading lady was Dorothy Johnson, who was not an older actress, but a young, robust eighteen-year-old who was a former beauty contest winner. During the filming, we became romantically involved and decided to go away for Labor Day weekend. We started toward Newport Beach on a Friday night, and, much to our dismay, every place we stopped at was booked. We drove a little further down the coast, and the story was the same. We drove to San Diego, now desperate for a room, but "no vacancy" signs were lit up all along the beach. We might as well have been in Las Vegas, there was that much neon. We finally decided that we'd drive back to my apartment in Los Angeles. We arrived back at 3:00 A.M.—tired yes, but not so tired we couldn't consummate our relationship.

Dorothy disappeared from the acting community, and I didn't hear from her again for another twenty-five years. My phone rang one day, and the voice over the phone said, "Edd, you'll never guess who this is."

"OK, I give up."

"Dorothy Johnson."

"DOROTHY JOHNSON?!"

I was happy to hear from her and was moved to ask, "What happened to you? Where have you been?"

She informed me that she had been living in Northern California and was going to be in Los Angeles the next week. Might we get together?

I met Dorothy for lunch. She was now in her forties, a little heavier, but still had that radiant, glowing smile that I remembered from when she was eighteen.

She got right down to business, "Edd, I want to get back into the movies."

Her husband had died recently, her children were all grown, and she was contemplating a return to acting. I tried to dissuade her.

"Dorothy, you don't want to do that. Forget about it. You don't know what the business is like now, and you don't want to know."

Her face was so sad, but I basically talked her out of it. We kissed good-bye, and I never heard from her again. That happens to so many actresses. They make a couple of movies, and they're gone. They just disappear. Hollywood is a very cruel town, especially for women. For men it's a little easier, but for women, it's downright brutal. A lot of actresses marry agents, business managers, directors, and producers for protection so that they don't have to deal with the brutality of show business.

After my first three movies, I got some work from Warner Brothers in a few television guest spots. I was dying to get that coveted, sacred seven-year contract, and I figured that if I didn't make my own breaks, nobody (and particularly my agent, now that I had turned him down cold) could do that for me. I decided that I would memorize every director, producer, and important executive's name to know who held some power in this town, anyone who had the authority to get me a seven-year contract.

One day I went over to the Warner lot to audition for a part on *Cheyenne*, the Western series starring Clint Walker. I read for producer Arthur W. Silver, a kindly older gentleman. He told me, "I really like you, Eddie, but I don't want you to do this role. I've got someone else in mind. There's an upcoming episode, and I think you'd really be good for that part." They were doing a remake of *Angels with Dirty Faces*, and they were calling it "The Brand." I was awarded the James Cagney role while Clint Walker got the Pat O'Brien role.

Before "The Brand" was aired, I made sure I knew who the man in charge of the television department was at Warner Brothers. His name was Mr. William T. Orr. Not only did I discover that Bill Orr was the head of television productions, but he was also Jack Warner's son-in-law, a man who held a lot of power at the studio.

The day after "The Brand" aired, I gathered together all of my friends, and we hunkered down and wrote a bunch of fan letters on my behalf and addressed them to Mr. William T. Orr. The letters and postcards were written in all kinds of different ink, different handwriting, and mailed out from locations all over the greater Los Angeles metropolitan area. I ended up spending around $100, but it turned out to be the single best investment of my life.

Because of all the fan mail that my friends and I sent in, mixed in with some legitimate letters that found their way to his office, Mr. William T. Orr was moved to call Jack Donaldson and ask, "Do you represent an actor named Edward Byrnes?"

"Yes, I do."

"This is Bill Orr at Warner Brothers. We'd like to offer Mr. Byrnes a seven-year contract. This kid has been getting fan mail like you wouldn't believe. We want to sign him. I think he has potential."

And that's the God's honest truth of how I got signed at Warner Brothers studio. Approximately one year later, I'd be getting those fifteen thousand fan letters a week, and they would be totally legitimate, more than any actor under contract.

That seven-year contract would later prove, in my case, that old adage, "Be careful what you wish for, it just may very well come true."

CHAPTER FOUR

Climbing to the Top

WARNER BROTHERS' contract was quite generous for a guy who never had anything in his whole life. The contract broke down as follows: $275 a week the first year; $350 a week the second year; $500 a week the third year; $750 a week the fourth year; $1,000 a week the sixth year; and finally, a maximum check of $1,250 a week for the seventh year. Warners had the option of canceling this arrangement annually. If an actor did not produce, or worse, was known as a troublemaker, the studio could dismiss him at the end of each six-month period. Basically, they had their actors by the balls.

During my first six months at Warner Brothers, they didn't know what to do with me, so they lent me to American International Pictures to make a less-than-memorable movie called *Reform School Girl* for $500 a week with a three-week guarantee. They were already making money off me.

The first picture I did for Warner, *Marjorie Morningstar*, in 1958, introduced me to a screen legend who would remain a friend until her untimely and sad death. Her name was Natalie Wood.

Natalie was very sweet and had the most gorgeous, brown, almond-shaped eyes that I have ever seen. We had a love scene together in the movie. Natalie was wearing a tight-fitting dress. The director, Irving Rapper, told me, "Now Edd, in this scene, you're really turned on by Natalie." Believe me, I didn't need much inspiration to be turned on by Natalie Wood. Natalie and I never became lovers.

Our friendship didn't flourish during the movie, and it wasn't until much later that we became very close friends.

A big thrill for me at the time was attending the premiere of *Marjorie Morningstar* at Radio City Music Hall and seeing my name up there in the screen credits with Gene Kelly and Natalie. If anything, it fueled my desire to succeed all the more.

Soon after that, I tested for *Darby's Rangers,* a film that was directed by the legendary director, William A. Wellman. Tab Hunter turned down the movie because he had just finished another Wellman picture, *Lafayette Escadrille.* I tested for it with Mr. Wellman directing me in a scene from the play *The Girl on the Via Flaminia,* and he awarded me the second lead in the film opposite James Garner.

Mr. Wellman was an Academy Award–winning director (*Wings)* and took an instant liking to me. He nicknamed me "Irish," for he knew that the name Byrnes was Irish, and that's what he called me for the rest of the picture. In return, I only called him Mr. Wellman because I had so much respect and admiration for him.

In his heyday, Wellman was called "Wild Bill" in Hollywood because he was known for his drinking escapades. He punched Spencer Tracy in the nose a few times when the two went out on a bender. Mr. Wellman was now well into his sixties, but he was still as spunky as ever. Executives endured "most" of his anger. They put up with his behavior, for after all, he did have a following and was a huge moneymaker for the studio.

When studio executives from Warner dropped by the set for a visit, Mr. Wellman would yell, "CUT! Hold everything. There are some suits here from the front office. Close it down." He did this right in front of them. Then he'd casually sit there in his director's chair, with his arms folded, and ask in a brash tone, "OK, you're holding up shooting. What do you want?" The executives backed off immediately and almost apologetically would say, "Oh, we're just dropping in to see how things are going." His answer, always curt, went something like this: "You don't have any business being here. We're working." These were the guys who buttered his bread, yet he treated them with much disdain.

This rebellious director sometimes had a .22 rifle within arm's reach. One day on the set I saw producer Martin Rackin coming, and I said, "Oh God, Bill's going to do something crazy." When the producer was close, William A. Wellman picked up the .22, carefully aimed at one of the studio lights, and fired. The light exploded, and the producer's forward motion stopped in an instant. He then slowly turned on his heel and walked back to his plush office never to be seen on the set again.

On another day, a studio guide quietly brought in a group of about twenty tourists—but not quiet enough. Wellman pulled aside two of the stuntmen and instructed them to fake a fight in the mud. The expletives and mud were flying all over the place, and it had the desired effect: the tourists scattered like rats on a sinking ship.

Etchika Chourea was an exotic-looking French woman who hardly spoke any English. Ms. Chourea was the leading lady in the picture, and I regret to this day not getting to know her as well as I would have liked. In addition to having a female interpreter who guarded her as a tiger would her cubs, we had problems with the language barrier. One thing was certain, we definitely had eyes for each other. I constantly tried to devise ways to make her interpreter/bodyguard disappear, but to no avail. I later heard that Etchika married an Arabian sheik. What did he have that I didn't, except maybe a few billion dollars and perhaps a seven-foot bodyguard experienced in dealing with overzealous French interpreters?

My career was kept busy after *Darby's Rangers,* and I was stuck in episodic limbo for a few months. I guest-starred on *Maverick* with James Garner three times. I also did *Lawman, Sugarfoot,* and *Cheyenne.* Westerns were the staple of American television then. I played mostly heavies, the "bad guys," which I loved. I also enjoyed getting dressed up, riding on horses, and fight scenes in saloons where I could put my acrobatic skills to good use.

The one memorable *Maverick* episode was with Lee Van Cleef, one of the great character actors of all time. When I walked onto the set, I heard this, "Psssssssssst, hey kid, kid."

I turned to look, and it was Lee hiding behind one of the buildings, waving me over. As I got within arm's reach, he handed me a flask.

"Have a drink."

I was twenty-two and didn't drink, but I was extremely polite. "Oh no, Mr. Van Cleef, that's OK. Thanks very much for the offer."

Lee Van Cleef, like most alcoholics, was a great person, but he had about three hours to kill in between shots and drank to pass the time. He had an assistant, and he'd have to be walked slowly to the set.

Later, Lee worked in Italy and Spain and became a big star in Europe. When I worked with him in his television series, *The Master,* in 1987, he was still drinking. He died two years later.

* * * * *

Girl on the Run written by Dean Hargrove was originally intended as a ninety-minute, low-budget B-movie about a singer who witnessed a murder. I played a professional hit man named Kenneth

Smiley, who had been contracted to find the singer and "take her out." Preceding my entrance on the screen, a special theme would be played adding that much more menace to my character. The audience shifted uncomfortably in their seats every time I zeroed in on the singer.

In the end, I was captured by the police, but remained defiant and cocky. Before the scene was filmed, the director told me to come up with a physical piece of business to let the police know that they hadn't broken my spirit. I began thinking about how George Raft flipped a coin in *Scarface* as a gimmick. So, when the scene began rolling, I smiled, casually took out my comb, and started combing my hair. A move that later became my worst nightmare.

The star, Efrem Zimbalist, Jr., played a private detective named Stuart Bailey. We made the picture in a couple of weeks and thought nothing more of it other than an additional film credit.

Warner Brothers showed a special sneak preview with all the executives in attendance at a Huntington Park theater along with a paying audience.

Efrem and I arrived at the preview together. We sat through the entire movie. When the curtain came down, we walked up the aisle to leave, but total chaos erupted when the crowd spotted us.

William T. Orr, Warner Brothers executive producer recalled, *"When the audience heard the eerie theme preceding the entrance of Byrnes's character, all the excitement started. The manager of our local station said, 'You'd better watch this kid.'"*

People at the preview were mobbing me, asking for my autograph, anything to get close to me. It was bizarre. Nothing like that had *ever* happened to me before. Executives were all watching; that included Bill Orr, Hugh Benson, and Roy Huggins. They were astounded. They probably said to themselves, *"What have we got here? They're mobbing this kid!"*

After signing autographs, Efrem and I had to be led to a limousine, and we were finally whisked away. It was a night that was to be repeated many times in the next several years, for I was both blessed and cursed with far more than my fifteen minutes of fame.

* * * * *

I was seeing Asa Maynor more and more, and we eventually became lovers. I still had affairs on the side, but Asa was more or less my main steady. When Asa was nineteen, I got her pregnant. We weren't married. I was broke, and I had no intention of marrying her at that time. We decided that an abortion would be the most logical choice given our situation. However, I vowed that I would not take Asa to get one in Mexico or from some back-alley butcher who used a coat hanger in place of a medical education. I explained our predicament one night to Michael and Dody Landon. At that point, Asa had not had her period for six or seven weeks, and we were both extremely nervous. Mike suggested a method requiring a gel that he could acquire from a doctor.

"A gel?" I inquired. "What kind of gel?"

Mike assured me the method was safe, and he invited us back to his house a few days later. As soon as Asa and I arrived, Mike held up a jarful of this greenish-blue-looking gunk for which I paid him fifty dollars.

Dody spread a sheet on the bed for Asa to lie on while I inserted the gel inside her. A few days later, Asa had her period. The mysterious substance had obviously done its job. That forced miscarriage was something that neither of us was proud of, but we felt it was the best solution given the circumstances. We were both very relieved.

I threw myself back into work and was cast in *Up Periscope,* a World War II adventure starring James Garner and Edmund O'Brien.

The movie featured several scenes in a submarine, and we did a majority of the filming in Coronado, just outside San Diego.

The director, Gordon Douglas, whom I admired tremendously, called me over during a lunch break. He wanted to tell me what a good job I was doing. As I sat there and listened, I had my face in my hands to cover my tears. After he finished congratulating and encouraging me, I began to weep uncontrollably.

"Eddie, are you all right? What's the matter?" the baffled director asked as he put his arm around me.

I managed to get out the words. "No man has ever talked like that to me before." And it was true. No man, especially my father, ever encouraged me and told me what a good job I was doing. A director's job is to make the actor feel comfortable in front of the camera, still I couldn't help it that day. I broke down and cried.

Getting a taste of stardom in *Girl On the Run* made me a little spoiled. I was to be billed fifth in *Up Periscope,* and I made my complaints to Bill Orr loud and clear. "Bill, you gave me a lead in *Girl on the Run* and now you give me this small role in *Up Periscope.* The worst part is, I have to share a dressing room with a guy named Warren Oates. Where the hell did that guy come from?"

Warren Oates only had a bit part in the film, and I thought it was a big inconvenience to share a hotel room with another actor. In addition, I wanted my privacy, and Warner Brothers was just being cheap by having everyone double up. Warren turned out to be quite a funny guy, but at the time, I was a city slicker, and he was definitely a country boy.

Gordon Douglas liked to have fun with Warren, who was playing a cook in the picture. Warren had a two-minute scene all by himself in which he was scrubbing dishes. Gordon told Warren to improvise and start talking to himself. As Warren started his soliloquy, the wily director surreptitiously arranged for everyone to tiptoe off the soundstage while Warren poured his heart and soul into the scene. When he was finished, Warren looked up to find that not one person had been around to see his gut-wrenching performance.

At that time, ABC Television was known as the "third" network, and its ratings ranked dead last. It desperately needed a hit series that would put it on the map.

When Bill Orr and Roy Huggins saw the audience reaction to *Girl on the Run,* they came up with the idea of turning the film into a series, thus making *Girl on the Run* a pilot. ABC ordered thirty episodes in hopes of a much needed television hit.

The minor inconvenience of having my character sent off to jail at the end of *Girl on the Run* didn't affect my chances of getting a role on the series. I was a shoo-in. People always ask me if there were any other actors up for the role of Kookie, and my answer has always been, "No. The role was created specifically for me."

The concept of the series, retitled *77 Sunset Strip,* was to mix suspense with light comedy and sex appeal. It was the first to use the boulevard of bright lights and cozy hideaways as a backdrop. It was also television's first hour-long detective series.

But the show had several other things going for it, adventure rather than hard-edged drama, the role of music to set the scene in the stories, and the catchy theme song by Mack David and Jerry Livingston. Who can forget the infectious beat of "*77 Sunset Strip . . . (click-click!)*"?

As far as demographics went, the show gave the older audience Efrem Zimbalist, Jr., and Roger Smith. For teenagers, there was the irresistible appeal of one Gerald Lloyd Kookson III, a.k.a. "Kookie."

It was the first show on television that parents and their children could watch together and equally enjoy. Everybody in the country stayed home on Friday nights to watch our program.

I was happy that I was now a part of a television series, but not happy that I was cast as a parking lot attendant. Not only that, but my character's name was "Kookie." What the hell kind of name was that? My part only required one or two scenes an episode at the most, so it was my intention to grab the audience's attention from the get-go. I had to think of ways to be noticed with the little airtime that I had.

First and foremost, since my character was supposed to be cool, he had to look cool. I remember that once, while attending the premiere of *Beneath the 12-Mile Reef* in New York, I spotted Robert Wagner walking into the theater wearing an overcoat, with the collar flipped up, revealing a red strip of velvet underneath. The overall effect was simple: he looked so much more dashing. Since the show was to be filmed in black and white, I ordered the wardrobe department to sew a black strip underneath the collar of my gray jacket. With the turned-up black collar, it would make me stand out all the more.

The other thing that I did was to incorporate my gymnastic skills into the dialogue. Those first few scenes with Efrem, I would swing around on a pole while talking to him. It not only made for a realistic scene, but it grabbed the audience's attention as well. I must say that the director, Richard L. Bare, was more than generous to listen to my suggestions and use them. It certainly could have been considered scene-stealing, but Efrem and Roger were comfortable letting me do my thing.

Lastly, I developed a schtick, a gimmick that became a double-edged sword later in my life—that damned comb!

I find it amusing now that combing my hair while talking to someone was what helped make me famous. If the shoe were on the other foot and someone started combing their hair constantly while I was having a conversation with them, I'd tell them, "Put the comb away. You're driving me crazy!"

I still wasn't comfortable with my acting. Underneath the cockiness was a frightened kid that no one saw. It was that cockiness and sheer determination that made me stay with the acting and, of course, wanting to become more successful than my father, who, in my mind, was a complete failure.

77 Sunset Strip debuted on October 10, 1958, and garnered a very respectable and sizable audience. The Nielsen ratings for that week showed the series attracted a 19.4 percent viewing, meaning that approximately twenty million people tuned in to watch the show.

I don't know what happened or how it happened, whether it was Edd Byrnes's jive-talking Kookie, the debonair Efrem Zimbalist, Jr., the charming Roger Smith, or the splashy and inventive plot twists the show came up with every week. Whatever the reason, within six weeks *77 Sunset Strip* was the hottest show on television. Our Nielsens went skyrocketing to a 38 percent share which almost doubled our audience to an astounding forty million people.

At the end of the first six weeks, I was receiving thousands of combs in the mail, fifteen thousand fan letters a week, and was an "overnight" sensation.

It was hard to imagine that little Eddie Breitenberger, ex-shoeshine boy, high-school dropout, and former male prostitute was now an international television star.

CHAPTER FIVE

Kookiemania

AT THE END of 1958, I was deluged with fan mail and requests for interviews. I was on the covers of six fan magazines a month. *Photoplay* named me the Most Outstanding Actor of 1959. "Television Today," an achievement panel of the television editors of United States, voted me the Most Promising Male Star of Tomorrow in *Fame's* Annual Critics Poll. *Who's Who In Television* named me the Best Actor in a Television Series. *Look* magazine voted me the Best Actor in an Action Series. For three years in a row, I was voted the Best Actor in a Series by the readers of *Bravo* magazine. The magazine's "Golden Otto" was one of Germany's most-coveted awards.

Accolades were pouring in, and my life was turning around. All about me was one continuous whirlwind of activity. Everybody came out of the woodwork to get a piece of "Kookie."

One of them was my first love, Inga Puthe, the one and the same Inga Puthe who had left me for dancer Tommy Wonder. I was invited as a guest to appear on *The Pat Boone-Chevy Showroom* in New York.

While staying at the Plaza Hotel, a huge crowd of screaming fans gathered in the lobby wanting to meet me. Inga managed to get producer Hugh Benson's attention and told him that she knew me.

"Edd, some gal named Inga Puthe is waiting outside for you. She said she's an old friend of yours," Hugh told me upon entering the room.

"Inga Puthe?" I yelled. I hadn't thought of her in years, but her name brought out an involuntary rage. I instructed Hugh to go downstairs and give my first love a message. "You tell Miss Puthe that I promised her one day she'd come crawling back to me. Also, tell her that I definitely *don't* want to see her. SEND HER AWAY!"

Now she wants me when I'm a hot television star, I thought.

I was immature, but I had my sweet revenge on Inga Puthe. I made sure she was paid back in spades for breaking my heart. It was mean, but she *had* hurt me so much.

In those days, we didn't have television shows like *Entertainment Tonight* or *Hard Copy*, so fan magazines served as the main promotional tool of stars. Warner had it set up so that I did an interview every workday of my life for five years, while I did *77 Sunset Strip*. During the hour lunch break, I had to shovel in my food while answering questions. The publicity department would tell me, "Edd, you have another interview today," and I'd just accept it. I didn't yet know how to say "no."

The studio spent hundreds of thousands of dollars publicizing me, something a young, unknown actor today would have to spend on his career out of his own pocket. When I went out in public, I was mobbed. I couldn't eat in a restaurant without someone approaching me and asking me in the middle of a meal, "Could I borrow your comb?" or "Can I have your autograph?"

When I went to a Las Vegas casino for some gambling, a crowd of thirty people or more would follow me around. If I played blackjack, I was the center of attention, and the people would cheer my every move. That can change a person.

I also made personal appearances and often traveled with Frank Casey, who was employed by Warner in the publicity department. The two of us ventured to Chicago for a personal appearance for the premiere of *Yellowstone Kelly.* I had a window seat on the plane. As we taxied off the runway, I noticed several thousand people (I was later told eighteen thousand) waiting on the tarmac. I commented to Frank, "Look at all of these people. President Eisenhower must be flying into town."

What Frank said next knocked me for a loop.

"Edd, those people aren't here to see the president of the United States. They're here to see you!"

"You must be joking! Me?"

Sure enough, thousands of teenagers screamed for my attention. I thought to myself, *This can't be for me!* The adulation I received surpassed any expectations in my wildest dreams. I constantly told myself, *This isn't happening to me. This can't be real.*

I discovered fame did have its little perks, and I fully intended to exploit each and every opportunity that presented itself to me. While on that same trip, I was invited to the Playboy Mansion, which was then headquartered in Chicago.

What doubled the fun was that Sammy Davis, Jr., was in town, and Sammy knew how to have a good time. I always stayed at the Ambassador East when in the Windy City, and the Playboy mansion was just around the corner.

Sammy and I arrived like giddy schoolboys on the doorsteps of the mansion. When we entered, it was every young boy's nocturnal fantasy come true. Hugh Hefner greeted us warmly and asked us to join the party. The women were not only plentiful, but all of them were dressed in very revealing evening gowns. The only suit in this place was a "birthday suit," and it wasn't my birthday or Sammy's the night we came to visit. Nude women were swimming in the indoor pool, and we couldn't believe our eyes. It was drinks, dancing, eating, and laughing. Fellini's *Satyricon* couldn't hold a candle to this place. The mansion was a twenty-four-hour party.

Hef could have been sleeping (although I don't know how with all of the action going on), and anyone could go into the kitchen and ask the cook at 2:00 A.M. to make eggs Benedict or whatever your pleasure might be. Hef was the ultimate host.

I did see quite a few of the bunnies at their best, but I never asked for any telephone numbers or dated anyone (except Asa) more than once because I thought the wine would always be flowing. I didn't want to limit my options of meeting other females. I wasn't interested in getting involved. Besides, I was working most of the time.

Another perk was meeting other celebrities, especially the ones that had been my heroes for years, namely, my "three godfathers."

The first time I met Kirk Douglas was at Natalie Wood's house when she was married for the first time to Robert Wagner. Kirk lived near their house and would walk through the alley with just his bathing suit on and no shirt. Kirk knew that I was once a gymnast and that gave us an immediate rapport. We tried to outdo each other with our gymnastic skills. Kirk could hold me up while I was in a handstand. No doubt about it, this middle-aged man was not only in great condition, he was very strong.

I witnessed firsthand the clout and power Kirk Douglas had in Hollywood when he arranged to get a print of a movie I made, *The Secret Invasion*, before it was even released. He invited me and Asa over to his house for dinner and for a personal viewing of the film in his screening room. That was a thrill!

When the movie finished, Kirk told me with all sincerity, "Edd, you really did a good job." I could have died that night with a smile on my face and called it a life.

I also witnessed, firsthand, the power of Kirk Douglas in Europe. I was in Rome, and Kirk and Anne Douglas happened to be there as well. I was leaving for Los Angeles the same day as the Douglases, and Kirk offered me a ride to the airport in his limousine.

We met at his hotel, and his driver headed out on this long stretch of country road. All of a sudden, we heard this siren in the distance. It was an Italian motorcycle cop, pulling over our vehicle for going a little too fast.

As the cop and the driver were speaking in Italian, I sat there wondering if Kirk would show his face to get his driver out of a ticket.

Kirk was sitting on the left-hand side of the car. He rolled down his window to give the cop a glimpse of his famous profile. When the cop spotted the movie star, his jaw dropped to the ground.

"Ah, see, Keerka Douglas, Keerka Douglas. I love-ah your movies." He then saluted Mr. Douglas and said to the limo driver, "Avanti! Avanti!"

The cop got back on his motorcycle, turned on his siren, and escorted us all the way to the Fiumicino Airport to make up for any lost time he may have caused. I was impressed.

As I got to know Kirk a little better, it stunned me that *he* believed he was still struggling to make it. If you've read his autobiography, *The Ragman's Son,* you'll understand: Kirk never got approval from his father. Kirk Douglas has probably accomplished more than any other living actor today, and yet he still thinks he hasn't "made it." I told him once, "Kirk, you don't need your father's approval. Why don't you just give yourself a pat on the back?"

Kirk is also enormously enthusiastic and ambitious. Once when we were both in London, he had his driver pick me up in his brand-new gray Rolls-Royce with red interior. Kirk was filming *Catch Me a Spy,* but he wanted me to go to lunch with him. On the way to the restaurant, he was reading the section of the newspaper covering all of the movies that had just opened in London. All of a sudden, he burst out, "Dammit! Marlon Brando got this part that I wanted." A few minutes later, the same thing, "Damn! Charlton Heston got this part that I wanted."

I offered, "Kirk, you can't be in every movie that's going to be made."

His reply: "Why not?"

The funniest anecdote I have about Kirk deals with when I was going to buy a new car, specifically a Jaguar. Kirk came along, and I asked him, "What do you think?" He commented, "It's beautiful."

"You ought to buy one, too." I told him.

"Nah, they're too expensive!"

My voice rose a notch or two, "You're Kirk Douglas! You could buy this whole showroom if you wanted. What do you mean, 'too expensive'?" I found it ironic. Kirk Douglas was content with his cars, but not with his career.

Asa had met Robert Mitchum at a party and told him that I really admired his acting and would love to meet him sometime. He was genuinely touched. A few months later, Asa and I were at LAX Airport getting ready to board when Bob came up to say hello. Asa introduced us. It turned out Bob was on the same flight, and we had a nice conversation on the plane. Afterwards I ran into him many times on the Warner Brothers lot. At that time, he was making the movie *Rampage.*

What many people don't know about Bob Mitchum is that he has a witty and wonderful sense of humor. He's an exciting and funny raconteur and can tell stories for hours on end. The last thing he wants to discuss is acting. Richard Widmark is a neighbor of his, and Bob likes to get together with Widmark because Dick hates talking about acting, too. Widmark loves making movies, but he just hates discussing acting.

Bob also has an ear for dialects. He does incredible imitations, as he proved in *Ryan's Daughter* when he played his role with an Irish accent. I was pleased when I met the celebrated screenwriter of the film, Robert Bolt, who also adapted the book *Dr. Zhivago*. Both were directed by David Lean.

I met Robert Bolt at Michael Caine's house in Windsor, England, years later. He told me that David Lean was too intimidated to ask Robert Mitchum to play the lead in *Ryan's Daughter*, so the task was given to Mr. Bolt to call Bob.

"Mr. Mitchum?" Bolt inquired on the phone.

A laid back, "Yeeeaaaahhhs," Mitchum replied.

"This is Robert Bolt, the writer. I'm associated with David Lean, the director."

"Yeeeaaaahhhs."

Wiping his brow, the writer continued, "We would like very much for you to come to Ireland and star in David's new film, *Ryan's Daughter*. Uhhmmm, what are you doing right now?"

"Uh, right now, I'm contemplating suicide," kidded the famous actor.

Bolt, without missing a beat said, "Well, Mr. Mitchum, would you mind putting that off for the time being until after you do the movie, and I'll be more than happy to pay for your funeral."

Bob laughed heartily and agreed to do the film.

I also found Bob to be a very kind and gentle man, which most people don't know. The public thinks of him as his screen persona, a tough guy, but he is very generous both with his time and his money. Many times I've had dinner with him, and he never once let me pick up the check.

The biggest thrill I've ever had with Bob was when I was invited to Mazatalan, Mexico, to give out trophies for a marlin-fishing contest. The sponsor of the contest would fly me and a friend out, house us in a villa overlooking the ocean, and pay all of our expenses, if I would hand out trophies for the biggest catch. My time would only involve a two-hour presentation for a free, fun-filled week.

I found out Bob happened to be there that same weekend and invited him for dinner one night. He came over to my table and entertained me with stories till 2:00 A.M. Finally, I had to tell him that I had to get to bed. I had an early morning call for marlin fishing. I then asked him to go with me. He responded in his inimitable voice, "Noooo. Pass. Nooo." So I asked, "Well, why don't you at least come to the party tomorrow night? We're smoking a marlin." Without so much as blinking an eye, he asked, "What kinda papers you gonna use?"

I told him how I didn't want to hand out trophies and that I was dreading the event. Bob offered, "Well, I'll help you." I told the sponsor that Robert Mitchum would be helping me and asked, "Would that be OK?" The man was beside himself with joy that the great actor would be participating in the event.

The night of the award ceremony, the 200 or so guests were appreciative. Bob was having fun and made everyone laugh. I'm sure it was the time of their lives, as it was mine. That was typical of Bob Mitchum's generosity.

Burt Lancaster will always have a warm place in my heart. He was such a genuinely nice and charming man. The last time I saw Burt before his death was at Chasens, a famous Beverly Hills restaurant where the stars liked to dine.

Troy Donahue called me one night and said his agent from Tokyo was in town with three friends from Japan. His agent was entertaining them, and they wanted to see some stars while in Los Angeles. I suggested Chasens and accompanied Troy and his guests. We were sitting in a booth, and the first person we saw was Frank Sinatra walking through the door and being seated at his table. I pointed and whispered to the ladies, "Frank Sinatra." Then, in walked Gregory Peck and his wife with Barbara Sinatra. I said to them, "I don't believe this! You wanted to see stars, and you're getting the crème de le crème of Hollywood at one table."

Our food arrived, and then I heard this familiar voice in the booth directly behind me. I was trying to place the voice, then all of a sudden it hit me: *Son of a gun, that's gotta be Burt Lancaster.* I leaned over, and sure enough, it was Burt entertaining a group of people with one of his stories. I didn't want to interrupt him, but I did want to say hello before he left.

As our group got up to leave, so did Burt's. After introducing the icon to our party, we started talking. I walked out with him and waited until the valet brought up his car, a four-door Jaguar. He turned to me and said, "It was great seeing you again, Edd."

"It was really good to see you, Burt."

He got in his car and drove off. I walked across the street to get into my car. As I inserted the key to unlock my car door, I was overcome by a wave of sadness. I got into the car, locked the door, and cried uncontrollably. I couldn't for the life of me figure out why I was so sad. Later, when I got into therapy and learned about John Bradshaw's theory of the inner child, I came to realize why I was so overcome with grief. *Once more, Burt Lancaster, my father, was abandoning me.* Little Eddie Breitenberger wanted him to take me home. The little kid inside of me who grew up without a father was being abandoned again. That was the last time I saw Burt Lancaster.

A few weeks later, Burt fell ill and went in for a seven-hour stomach operation. I sent him a telegram wishing him well. He must have been uplifted by my good wishes because he had his secretary call me later. She said, "Burt's been trying to get your address to send you a thank-you letter. He was so touched by your telegram, but he didn't know your address."

A few days later, I received his letter. It read:

Dear Edd,

Many many thanks for your wire and expression of concern. As you must know, I had a pretty rough time of it for awhile. I'm not quite ready for the "highbar" but I'm pleased to tell you that I'm on the mend.

I plan to be leaving for Italy in two weeks to visit my daughter, who lives in Rome. By the time I return, sometime in the spring, I should be back at full strength and I promise you that I will take another crack at that highbar.

Again, thanks for your thoughtfulness.

Sincerely,
Burt

He later suffered a stroke and never was the same man again. I ran into Kirk Douglas in Beverly Hills one day while he was walking his dog, or should I say, the dog was walking Kirk. The canine was so huge that it was actually pulling Kirk down the street. To say the least, it was comical.

I pulled up the car and chatted with Kirk. We got on the subject of Burt's health, and I asked him, "Have you seen him?"

Kirk replied, "No, but I want to. His family won't let anyone see him. I have to respect their wishes."

It obviously hurt Kirk not to see Burt because the two men loved each other enormously, like brothers. They made five films together and grew very close as a result.

I ran into Burt's daughter one night at a party and asked about her father. She said, "He's watching a lot of his old movies that he hasn't seen in forty years. He's getting a real kick out of them."

When Burt finally died, I didn't cry, but I certainly felt a loss. I don't know if I've really accepted his loss or mourned for him yet. I don't think it's hit me. The first thing I did when I heard of his demise was to pray and then watch one of my favorite movies of his, *The*

Crimson Pirate. Why that particular movie? That was when Burt was at his peak, where he looked so young, handsome, and strong, at the top of his game. That's the Burt Lancaster I choose to remember.

* * * * *

The Complete Directory To Prime Time Network TV Shows wrote, "It was Kookie who caught the public's fancy and propelled the show into the top ten. Byrnes soon began to overshadow the series' principals as a popular celebrity, a kind of 'Fonzie' of the 1950's."

One of the reasons why people stayed up to watch the show was to hear the jive-talk that Kookie would spew from his mouth from week-to-week, known affectionately as "Kookie-isms." For nostalgia buffs, here's a list of Kookie-isms that took the country by storm:

KOOKIE-ISM	TRANSLATION
I've got smog in my noggin	I'm losing my memory
Buzzed by germsville.	Put into the hospital
Stabling a horse	Parking a car
Piling up the Zs	To sleep
Keep the eyeballs rolling	Be on the lookout
Play like a pigeon	Deliver a message
A dark seven	A depressing week
Headache grapplers	Aspirin
Baby, you're the ginchiest!	You're the coolest!

Did Mr. Edward Byrnes know what the "ginchiest" meant or any other "Kookie-ism" that was brought up in script meetings? I didn't have the faintest idea what they were talking about.

The idea for the jive talk cannot be pinpointed to one man. If it could, that man would have last been seen wearing cement shoes or on a one-way trip to the middle of the Sahara Desert or being dragged by a horse through the world's largest cactus patch or perhaps being thrown into a den of starving lions that hadn't been fed in a week . . . well, you get the idea.

The show had several writers on the staff, and every week they'd come in with some cockamamie word or phrase they invented. I'd look at them and say, "Baby, you're the ginchiest? Where do you get this stuff?" It was total nonsense, and when I'd say it on the show, all of a sudden it became a national buzzword. To all of the English teachers who taught teenagers, let me take this opportunity to apologize for butchering the English language. Honestly, *I* didn't make that stuff up.

First and foremost, I never, *ever* talked that way. Second, the only way to keep those speeches in my head was to learn them word by word, which made my job as an actor that much tougher.

Many times people would come up and start talking to me, inject a Kookie-ism here and there and wait for my response.

"Pardon me?" I would answer. "What did you just say?"

It's amazing what people will remember you for.

I couldn't comprehend why there was such an interest in me or my alter ego, Kookie. People went berserk wherever I appeared. I was suddenly cast into a world that I didn't fully understand or appreciate.

Coming from my background, I was ill equipped to deal with the situation and sought answers not in God or any other religious figure. No, my answer was the upcoming sixties credo that boldly proclaimed: "If it feels good, do it!"

CHAPTER SIX

Hollywood Nights

THE SECOND year of *77 Sunset Strip* kicked into high gear when the show's season premiere featured Kookie helping Stu Bailey catch a jewel thief by staging a revue in which I sang a song called, "Kookie, Kookie, Lend Me Your Comb." In its second year, the show was more popular than ever. It climbed into the number six spot overall and was number one in its time slot.

While the words to "Kookie, Kookie, Lend Me Your Comb" wouldn't exactly leave Lennon and McCartney shaking in their boots, the song proved to be enormously popular. It reached as high as number four on the *Billboard* magazine's charts and eventually ended up selling two million copies.

When production for the new season was getting underway, I had received a call from Hugh Benson, Bill Orr's right-hand man. He proclaimed, "You're going to make a record."

I almost gagged. "What?"

He continued with what I most assuredly thought was a joke. He said, "You're going to make a record for Warner Brothers."

I objected, "Hugh, I don't know how to sing."

He calmly stated, "That's OK. You're going to talk this song through like Rex Harrison did on *My Fair Lady.*"

At least Rex Harrison had some pizazz with his accent. I had just gotten rid of my New York accent a few years before.

Hugh also added, "Connie Stevens will do the singing, and you'll just fill in the other half of the song by talking."

"I will?"

A few days later, Connie Stevens and I were in the recording studio. I spent about five hours at the session, while Connie, bless her heart, spent *a lot* more time and effort than I on the song.

To this day, I contend that "Kookie, Kookie, Lend Me Your Comb" was the first rap song. It was rap! White rap, but nonetheless, I made the record some thirty-odd years before Vanilla Ice became popular.

I got 5 percent of the novelty hit and ended up making around eighty thousand dollars from the sales of the record because I signed a contract with Warner Brothers Records. They only paid me the royalties in portions, ten thousand here, twenty thousand there, over a period of two years. They were afraid that if I got the money in a lump sum, I might leave the series as Tab Hunter had done after cutting a hit record. Tab made a small fortune and left Warner Brothers high and dry when he had enough of them. Warner didn't want a repeat performance from me.

Connie Stevens is a nice Brooklyn girl, and today we are still friends. The interesting thing about the song was that she was never paid a cent of royalties because she wasn't signed with Warner Brothers Records. She basically sang the song, and I was the one who collected royalties. I also received a gold record, but Connie never got one for her effort.

We both performed the song on Dick Clark's *American Bandstand* in New York City before a first-time live audience. Connie and I lip-synched the number, but we couldn't hear ourselves. The audience noise was absolutely deafening.

After we finished the song, it was total mayhem trying to get out of the theater. The police had to escort us through the rabidlike fans into our limousine. Once we were in, the fans crowded the street behind the theater and left us with no place to go. Then all of a sudden, they were on the hood, on the roof, faces looking in the windows, rocking the limo back and forth, screaming their little prepubescent heads off. It gave me the chills because it was as if they were yelling for someone else. It was different; like nothing I had ever experienced before. This fame business was beginning to rear its ugly little head.

One nice thing that I did get to do was to fly in my family from New York to visit Los Angeles. I sent first-class tickets to my mother, sister, and Nana. They visited me on the set and had their pictures taken with Efrem Zimbalist, Jr., and Roger Smith, and any other star who may have been walking around on the Warner Brothers lot.

It was payback time to the three special ladies in my life, especially Nana, who was always so good to me. Secretly, I wanted to make good to her ever since I was ten years old. One time when she wasn't looking, I stole a five-dollar bill that she had stashed underneath her carpet. As petty as that might have seemed, I had been carrying around the guilt all those years, and I tried to make it up to her ever since.

I am constantly being asked by fans of the series how the three stars of *77 Sunset Strip* got along, Efrem Zimbalist, Jr., Roger Smith, and me. The answer has always been the same: famously.

I can honestly say that there was no jealously on their part regarding my popularity. Yes, my part was the flashy role, but the two men became very good friends and were secure enough with themselves that they didn't have to be jealous of my success. They were having their own. They may even have been sympathetic toward my plight because they saw the craziness that surrounded my life.

Efrem Zimbalist, Jr., is one of the finest men you'd ever want to meet and was already an established star when the series became a hit. He didn't have any reason to be jealous of my success.

Roger Smith and I became very close friends, and he was genuinely happy for me. He built a wine cellar one summer in my bachelor pad in Coldwater Canyon and served as the best man at my wedding.

A typical day in the life for me at that time consisted of a wake-up call by the assistant director, Rusty Meek. Rusty was good about not calling me four hours before I had to get to the set. I had pulled him aside one day and said, "Rusty, I live twenty-two minutes away from the studio, so give me a call an hour before I have to report to makeup." And he did, which made my life that much easier.

I had no set pattern when I had to come to work. I'd work, have lunch, do interviews with the fan magazines, go back to work, and call it quits by 7:00 P.M. Then it was time to play.

Roger Smith and I occasionally got off work early in the afternoons. We'd drop by a talent school on Hollywood Boulevard and make our presence known to all of the would-be actresses and dancers of tomorrow.

One of these aspiring young actresses was the beautiful Peggy Lipton who starred a few years later on *The Mod Squad.* Peggy was sixteen and quite shy. Her only request was to keep the lights off while we made love. Peggy also stuttered, but somehow cured herself of that impediment on her way to becoming successful actress. I believe that Peggy, now in her forties, is much more attractive than she ever was.

Roger Smith was first married to Victoria Shaw, a beautiful actress from Australia. Victoria was under contract at Columbia and starred in *The Eddie Duchin Story.* Asa and I were very close friends with the Smiths. Roger was not as wild as I, but he was game for anything suggested. Since I was the naughty boy of the bunch, one night I recommended, after a couple of bottles of wine, that we switch partners. Roger, Victoria, Asa, and I took off all our clothes and got into bed. (This was years before *Bob and Carol and Ted and Alice* hit the movie theaters.) For some reason, when we started to get into it, we looked at each other and began laughing so hard that we couldn't go through with it.

A similar situation arose (no pun intended) another time at Natalie Wood's house when someone suggested we have an orgy. Natalie was with Arthur Lowe at the time. Jill St. John was accompanied by her first husband, Lance Reventlow, the son of heiress Barbara Hutton. Asa and I rounded out the party roster. We were all drinking white wine and either from embarrassment or the heavy influence of alcohol, we couldn't go through with it. We did, however, always end up nude in Natalie's sauna.

Nude-swimming parties were also quite normal for the six of us. We didn't have sex, but we found it very relaxing and thought nothing of being naked in front of each other. Lance owned a palatial home in Beverly Hills and built a bar that connected to his swimming pool. We could swim under a partition into the living room.

It was certainly a fun time. We were all young and good looking. The wine was flowing, and the money was rolling in. Any fantasy that I ever imagined as a kid had all started to come true.

Speaking of nude swimming, actor Rod Taylor lived directly below me in Coldwater Canyon. We became pretty good friends. He was a very congenial host and loved to play the role of bartender whenever he had Asa and me over.

Rod had various houseguests that stayed at his place, but the one I remember best was that well-endowed Swedish actress, Anita Ekberg.

You movie fans may remember her in *La Dolce Vita*, bathing in Rome's Trevi Fountain. One sunny morning, I was having breakfast on my balcony, which overlooked Rod Taylor's swimming pool. Anita liked to swim and sunbathe topless. Being from Europe, she was not ashamed to show off her body, and she yelled up to me, "Edd, dahling, how are you?"

"Wonderful," I responded, watching her jiggle in all the right places.

It was the good life.

* * * * *

I discovered that *77 Sunset Strip* was not only popular in the United States, but in England, Germany, Japan, Spain, and all over the world. For some reason unbeknownst to me, the show was enormously popular in Germany. The show really took off there. When I won the Golden Otto Award for Best Actor in a Television Series, I flew to Germany to receive the award in person. For the photo shoot, the photographer for the magazine came up with the brilliant idea to have me pose with seventy-seven teenagers that were fans of mine. I arrived by limo and was mobbed German-style. The only thing different than getting mobbed American-style was that I couldn't understand what they were screaming. The photographer tried to hold them back, but they were so wild that I had to dive back into the limousine in fear for my life. The photographer never did get the shot. The hysteria there was only comparable to what Elvis or the Beatles suffered.

Speaking of Elvis, I got to know the King on a social level when he was on the set at Paramount doing all of those musicals. He'd periodically come over to me and say hello. He was superfriendly, and I felt no competition from him as a fellow teen idol. Maybe it was because he knew I couldn't sing a lick.

The last time I saw Elvis, he was headlining at the Hilton Hotel in Las Vegas in the late sixties. I was with Asa and Joan Collins, watching the show from a booth. In the middle of his act, the big E announced, "Ladies and gentlemen, there's a special friend of mine in the audience tonight. Please say hello to Mr. Edd Byrnes." I didn't even know that Elvis knew that I was in the audience, and

I was deeply touched by his introduction. Joan Collins was certainly impressed. (I later found out from a book on Elvis that he routinely sent out "the Memphis Mafia" to search out the crowd for celebrities and report it back to him. Oh well, I still felt special that evening by his kind gesture.)

At the end of his show, Elvis sent over one of his people and asked if we'd like to come up and visit with him in his suite. We were escorted through the kitchen and up a back elevator into his penthouse suite. A couple of his entourage were there, and he came out with a towel around his neck.

Elvis gave me a warm greeting, and I introduced him to Asa and Joan. He gave Joan a big hug and a kiss, and she practically fell over. I had never seen Joan Collins blush from being so thrilled about any man, and that includes Warren Beatty!

Priscilla was there as well, and after Elvis excused himself, she told a story that I found quite amusing. Many times throughout his performance, Elvis would give away these expensive fifty-dollar silk scarves to the fans in the audience. Priscilla found this act of charity to be too expensive, so she shopped for similar-looking scarves and found some for only five dollars. She proudly held up her five-dollar bargains and announced, "Look, they're almost the same thing."

The biggest shame to me about Elvis was that he was a fine actor. He was offered a lot of good movies, but Colonel Tom Parker shot them all down because Elvis was paid a flat fee of a million dollars to star in musicals, not dramas that required real acting. Elvis Presley was the first person to be offered *Sweet Bird Of Youth*, the part Paul Newman eventually played. I always thought Elvis would have been terrific in that movie.

I began to hang out more and more with Holmby Hill's "Rat Pack." Sammy Davis, Jr., loved *77 Sunset Strip* and was especially a big fan of mine. Sammy used to talk that hip jive talk for real. He asked to have a guest spot written in for him, and the producers were more than happy to comply. He really wanted to do the show. He was in Las Vegas performing on the Strip, and his last show ended around midnight. He climbed into the back of his limousine to sleep while his driver headed straight to the Warner Brothers studio in Burbank for a 7:00 A.M. makeup call. The show he did was one of the most memorable episodes of the series.

When I think of Sammy Davis, Jr., I think of rum and Coke. That was his drink. He had a rum and Coke in one hand and a cigarette in the other. Just like his stage act. His life was onstage.

Sammy was one of the most lovable people I have ever had the pleasure to know. I think he desperately wanted people to love him. If he had one flaw, it was that he had to be "on" all the time. Sammy was a expert with a quick draw and practiced many many hours. He could pull out his guns, twirl them back and forth, catch them, and put it back in his holster. The man was so full of life.

When I was in New York, I had a birthday party at the famous Little Club, and Sammy Davis, Jr., and Bobby Darin were there to help me celebrate. It was one of those periods in my life where I could have met anyone I wanted just by picking up the phone. I was living a charmed life.

Through Natalie and R. J. Wagner, I met Frank Sinatra. Frank would drop by their house for an occasional drink. I later moved near his place on Bowmont Drive, and he'd drive by and say, "Hi, neighbor." I never found Frank to be the intimidating guy portrayed in the media. Although, he did have a sign on his front gate that read: "If you haven't been invited here, get the hell out!"

After Frank got to know me a little bit better, he asked me to introduce him at a charity concert he was going to do at Soldier's Field in Chicago. A record-breaking eighty thousand people showed up, and I had never seen anything like this before in my life. I went with Sammy, Frank, and Peter Lawford. We all stayed at the Ambassador East. Frank booked Peter and me separate rooms and a two-bedroom suite for him and Sammy. Upon entering their suite, I noticed a very pungent smell and said to myself, *This is not cigarette smoke.* I found it not only ironic, but quite funny that these two master showmen would get a little high before going onstage in the name of charity.

All of us piled into a limousine, and once at Soldier's Field we were escorted by the police to the dressing room. Peter Lawford warmed up the crowd, and then he introduced me to the screaming sea of fans. We did a little routine before introducing Frank. He brought down the house.

Later on during the encore, Frank, Sammy, Peter, and I came on stage to perform a number. As I was singing, it hit me, *I'm on stage with Frank Sinatra and Sammy Davis, Jr. Somebody wake me up.*

When the show was over, we piled into the limo and headed to the Ambassador Hotel. We were all pretty tired by the time we got back to the hotel, but Frank decided then and there he wanted a world-famous Chicago hot dog. When Frank Sinatra decides to get a hot dog, *everybody* has to get one. So it was back into the limo in search of the perfect weenie. This was around 2:00 A.M. in the late fifties and on a weeknight. The town wasn't exactly open for business at that hour, but Frank was determined. He'd pull up to strangers walking on the street and ask, "Yo, pally. Where can we find the best hot dog in town?" It was bizarre—four famous people in a limousine, asking complete strangers where to find the best hot dog in town. We finally did find an all-night deli, and Frank savored his hallowed Chicago-style weenie before calling it a night.

Since I did bring up the Rat Pack and Peter Lawford, I must admit I found him to be a very strange guy.

I remember once Asa and I followed him to his house on Pacific Coast Highway in Santa Monica. Peter liked to play practical jokes, but he possessed a very weird sense of humor. We were all drinking that night and around 3:00 A.M., he wanted to pull a prank on his agent, Milt Ebbins. Milt was a very famous and powerful agent and unfortunately, was the main recipient of Peter's bizarre sense of humor.

"We have to play a gag on Milt," Peter ordered.

Peter came up with this idea that I would call Milt, tell him that Peter was in jail, and that he needed him to bail him out.

I dialed the number and Milt answered the phone as if awoken from a deep REM sleep. "Hello?" answered the weary agent.

"Milt, Edd Byrnes here. I just left Peter and he's in jail. You gotta come over and bail him out."

I proceeded to embellish this story with a few details, and Milt was tearing his hair out. Peter was in the background egging me on to tell more sordid lies, to keep the fire burning and say anything outrageous that might give poor old Milt a heart attack.

Milt believed everything I told him (after all, I am an actor), and he was practically on the verge of a nervous breakdown when Peter whipped the receiver away from my hand and yelled into the mouthpiece, "AHA! MILT! It's Peter. I'm just pulling your leg! I'm not in jail, old chap."

Over the phone I could hear Milt scream, "PETER, WHAT THE FUCK ARE YOU DOING CALLING ME UP AT THREE IN THE MORNING AND WAKING ME UP?"

That was Peter Lawford in a nutshell.

Two weeks before he died, I saw Peter Lawford at a 12-step meeting. I did not recognize him. I was behind him and when he turned around, it was not the same Peter that I had known. He had become so thin and had aged terribly. He had a yellow pallor to his skin and looked like he was at death's door. It was a sad deterioration of a man who had once possessed all of the Great American Dream. He died of cirrhosis of the liver.

One of the most disappointing things that happened to me during this period was when I was living on Bowmont Drive and was sick in bed with a cold. It was around eight at night when the phone rang. It was Roger Smith.

"Edd, it's Roger. Cagney wants to meet you."

"You're kidding? He does?"

Roger was a good friend of James Cagney. It was Cagney who discovered Roger on the set of *Man of a Thousand Faces* before our series ever started. Cagney had seen *77 Sunset Strip*, and the two men were talking about the show. Mr. Cagney was curious about me. Roger offered to make an introduction.

"Yeah, Cagney wants to meet you. We're right down the hill from you on Coldwater Canyon, only a few minutes away."

"God, Roger, I feel lousy tonight. I'm in bed with a cold."

It was one of those moments in my life I wish I could take back. I should have just dragged myself out of bed and gotten dressed, but I was too sick to get in my car and meet the legend. I felt that there would always be another time, another place, but I never did get to meet James Cagney.

The strongest friendship that I forged at this stage was with Natalie Wood, but it was Robert Wagner who first extended his friendship.

During the summer break in the series, I was offered the second lead in a Western called *Yellowstone Kelly,* starring Clint Walker.

While on the soundstage filming, I received a phone call. One of the assistant directors told me that Robert Wagner wanted to talk to me.

I always thought of R. J. as a big movie star and was flattered that he called to talk to me.

"Edd, it's R. J. Wagner."

"Hi, where are you?"

"I'm on the lot. Can I come over and see you?"

"Great! C'mon over."

We talked and exchanged phone numbers. I asked him about his clothes because he always looked like a million bucks. R. J. took me under his wing and introduced me to his tailor, a little Italian guy by the name of Ernie Tarzia on Vine Street. Ernie made all of R. J.'s suits, and in time, he became my tailor as well. That little gesture seemed to cement our friendship. Our relationship continued after he married Natalie Wood. When I had first introduced Asa to Natalie, the two hit it off like long-lost friends.

In the early days of R. J. and Natalie's divorce, Asa and I must have spent nearly four days a week at Natalie's house on North Bentley Drive. Natalie employed a housekeeper who didn't know how to cook, so the menu was always the same: salad, baked potato, and a steak, and of course, lots of wine.

R. J. and Natalie were a great couple. They were not only very glamorous, but charming as well. This didn't mean that they were immune to fights.

Natalie left R. J. when she made the film *Splendor in the Grass* with Warren Beatty. I was quite surprised when Natalie made that decision, because Warren at the time was not one you would define as a "real catch." He had a bad complexion, was quiet and shy, had none of R. J.'s charisma, and wasn't working that much. I do know that when he and Natalie were living together, she was paying all the bills.

Life with Natalie was always exciting, if not downright dramatic at times. She once had a boyfriend from Venezuela, named Ladislav ("Ladi") Blatnik. Ladi was a very quirky guy. Once Asa and I were at Natalie's for dinner when she announced like an excited teenager, "Ladi's going to be calling from Caracas tonight at ten."

Ladi's call came through at ten on the dot, and when they were finished talking, Natalie hung up the phone. We were sitting in her living room when I saw this person running across her lawn. It was like a flash, but I saw something in her backyard. With a great flourish, Ladi opened up the side door and announced to everyone in the room, "I'm here!" He surprised Natalie and took her into his arms, making one of the all-time grand entrances, certainly any actor or actress could appreciate that.

A couple of times a year, Asa and I would stay in Palm Springs with Ladi and Natalie. At the end of their relationship, they were fighting all the time.

On one occasion, the four of us were having a drink toward the end of the night. I announced, "I'd really like to get a good night's sleep. Does anyone have a sleeping pill?" Natalie said, "Yeah, Edd, just a second."

She disappeared into her bedroom and after a few minutes, came back out and handed me the biggest pill I had ever seen in my life. I looked at the long, cylindrical pill in amazement and told Natalie, "I can't swallow this. It's too big!"

My most gracious hostess told me, "Stick it up your ass."

"Excuse me?" I asked, not thinking I heard her correctly.

Natalie laughed, "It's a suppository. It's a sleeping pill. You stick it up your ass. It gets into your bloodstream much faster that way."

That next night, I was in bed sleeping when Natalie threw open my door and cried out, "Eddie, Ladi's trying to kill himself. He's swallowed a whole bottle of sleeping pills."

Natalie called the paramedics while I went looking around for the empty bottle to give the paramedics a clue as to what to do when they arrived.

I rifled through the medicine cabinet and found nothing. I then spotted a few pills at the bottom of the toilet bowl and realized that Ladi must have flushed most of the pills down the toilet. I told Natalie of my finding, and Ladi finally came clean.

"I didn't swallow the pills. I just wanted to fake a suicide to get Natalie to feel sorry for me and take me back," he admitted, as he tried to play on her emotions.

Ladi was forever taking Natalie on trips and buying her flowers and spending lavish amounts of money on her. He told her that he was a millionaire in Venezuela and owned a very successful shoe factory.

We were to discover that Ladi came to the United States for the sole purpose of wooing Natalie Wood off her feet and marrying her. His friends from Venezuela financed his trips to the tune of approximately ten thousand dollars per visit, and Ladi promised he would reimburse them when he had married the movie star. The sad thing was, it almost worked. Natalie finally caught on to him and broke off their engagement.

I remember R. J. was heartbroken when he and Natalie got divorced the first time. R. J. asked me to take him to the airport when he decided to go to London and film *The War Lover* with Steve McQueen.

Feeling that R. J. needed a shoulder to cry on, I just drove and listened to my friend. "I'm leaving her everything and taking only whatever I'm wearing," R. J. said in a somber tone.

Somehow or another, McQueen's agent managed to finagle top billing over R. J., which baffled me because R. J. was a much bigger star. I asked R. J. how he felt about that, and he revealed, "I don't like it, but it was offered to me, and it was a chance to get away and get my mind off of Natalie."

R. J. and Natalie's relationship was typical of how the small town of Hollywood could make it appear as if everything was perfect, on the face of it, but anyone caught up in the trap, the half-truth of the place, could easily go to hell in a handbasket.

The same could be said for my relationship with Warner Brothers and the series. That second year on *77 Sunset Strip* was truly a high point in my career, but the year to come would reveal how fast things can take a nosedive for an actor.

Nineteen sixty would prove to be the hardest year of my life.

CHAPTER SEVEN

Contract Dispute

IT HAD BEEN the accepted rumor that I left *77 Sunset Strip* because the producers of the show would not expand my role.

To this, my unequivocal response is "ABSOLUTELY NOT TRUE!"

My role was expanded only six weeks after the show premiered. I was a big draw, and there simply was no reason to ask for a bigger role. (Besides, I didn't want to work that hard.) Wanting more lines would seem to imply that there was jealousy on the set, and as I have stated, before the cast got along famously.

My problem was simply money and missed film opportunities. After three years, I was still getting what my contract stated I would receive, $500 a week. The guest stars that made appearances were getting a flat $750 a week, and they were relative unknowns.

I was also flooded with film offers from other studios, but Warner wouldn't budge. I would regularly get offers of $250,000 a movie. Even by today's standards, that was serious money. In fact, it would be equal to five million dollars for a film today.

There's a wonderful story that actor Richard Harris tells often regarding an exchange he had with the famous and mighty mogul, Jack L. Warner. Harris had done *Camelot* on Broadway and in 1967, he went to the Warner Brothers lot to make the film. In the play, Lady Guinevere and Sir Lancelot do not consummate their relationship. In the film version, they do. Richard Harris balked at the idea that sex was needed to sell this picture to the movie-going public. He spoke his piece to Jack L. Warner in his office, and the head of the studio listened intently and politely to what Mr. Harris had to say. When Harris was finished, Jack L. Warner held up his finger and said quietly, "Would you please follow me."

"Where are we going?" asked Harris.

"Please follow me," said the mysterious man who headed the studio.

Mr. Warner walked the actor through long corridors, through the parking lot, and out past the front gates, where the two men had a perfect view of the Warner Brothers Studio water tower.

"Mr. Harris," said Jack L. Warner, "would you please tell me what that water tower says."

"It says Warner Brothers Studio," replied "King Arthur."

"That's right. Warner Brothers Studio," said Mr. Warner, rather curtly. "When it says Harris Brothers Studio, then you can tell me my *fucking* business. Now go make my movie!"

I, too, would have several "exchanges" with Mr. Jack L. Warner.

Frank Sinatra wanted me for *Ocean's 11*. I went to Jack Warner's office to plead to his business side, "Look, if I'm in a movie with Frank Sinatra, it will bring more attention to the series, and it will make more money for Warners than the actual show." He wouldn't go for it.

Twentieth Century-Fox wanted me for *North to Alaska*, the part that eventually went to Fabian. Again, I went up to see Jack Warner and said, "Jack, 20th Century-Fox has offered me a movie with John Wayne. John Wayne, Jack!" He calmly said, "Nope. No, forget it." *Rio*

Bravo was another movie starring Duke, but this time the producing studio was none other than Warner Brothers. I thought for sure I was a shoo-in. I expressed my interest to Jack Warner to play the young gunslinger in the film. "Look, I'm begging you. Please let me do this picture. John Wayne. Dean Martin . . . " That was one picture I *desperately* wanted to do. Again, it was the same old story. "Edd, you have the series to do." They gave the part to Rick Nelson.

Darryl F. Zanuck sent me a telegram to inquire if I would be interested in making *The Longest Day,* a classic World War II film that eventually saved 20th Century-Fox from bankruptcy and made everyone in it a star to boot. To go up to Jack L. Warner's office again and plead with him to do this movie would be like doing the same thing over and over again, but this time, I was expecting different results.

I began building up a big resentment toward Mr. Jack L. Warner. I felt that he was putting up a major roadblock to my film career, and also through the process, he was negatively affecting my financial future. Who knows how long an actor will be hot? You have to grab that brass ring when you get the chance. In retrospect, that was my chance.

For three years, Warner had made millions off of my name. I brought millions of viewers to the show, had a hit record, and costarred in two hit movies. My face graced several magazine covers a month, I received thousands of letters of fan mail, but worst of all, I made publicity appearances on behalf of the show and never got paid for them. Warner Brothers would collect and pocket the usual ten thousand dollar fee for an appearance, and I never saw a dime. Not once did Jack ever say, "Edd, you're doing a great job. Here's a ten-dollar bonus." Not once.

Granted, the contractual $500 a week was excellent money for the time. There was also the situation of living beyond my means. I bought a brand new home, a fancy foreign sports car, tailor-made suits, and I began to collect fine wines. In addition to that, I was supporting my mother and sister in New York. When I signed my seven-year contract, I made sure they got out of that run-down apartment. I had them moved into a posh uptown building, complete with a doorman in uniform, which in New York City, translates to "respectability."

This was not the first time a contract dispute arose at Warner Brothers. James Garner refused to go to work on *Maverick* as did Clint Walker on *Cheyenne.* James Cagney, whose name appeared above the title in *The Public Enemy*, was under contract for $350 a week. Warner Brother's policy was always the same: "Not a penny more!"

Jack Warner really had nothing to do with signing me, that was Bill Orr's doing, but Jack ran the studio, and the buck stopped with him. Jack could approve of a raise, or let me go off and do a few movies if he so desired.

When the series took off, Jack Warner often invited me to his private dining room that came complete with a kitchen, a gourmet chef, and waiters sporting white gloves. The studio mogul had slicked-back hair, a pencil-thin mustache, and was always impeccably dressed. Mr. Warner was also a commissioned colonel in the army, and he loved to be addressed as "Colonel." Everyone either called him J. L. or Colonel, but never Jack. He also had a fleet of cars on the lot but surprisingly never had a chauffeur or limousine. He preferred driving his black Bentley. Here's a bit of trivia: His car tires were always blackwalls. He had a strange aversion to those gangster whitewalls. Maybe he had one too many run-ins with the Mafia in his day. Who knows?

In a desperate last-ditch attempt to get a raise, I went to Jack's office a third time and tried to talk to him, "mano a mano."

Jack did a magnificent job of avoiding the business at hand. He enjoyed telling jokes, and he preferred to keep the conversation light. Jack hated confrontations, but he was going to get one this day.

"Colonel, I've got my mother and sister living in New York. I'm their only means of support. My brother never sends them a cent. I'm getting all these generous movie offers, and I can't make any of them. Why don't you, at the very least, just give me a raise?"

His response was typical Jack Warner, "You're such a young kid. What do you need money for?"

I reiterated my story for him. "My mother and sister need my financial support in New York. In addition, I just bought a new house and car. I really could use the money." I gave the man my most heartfelt, impassioned speech. It was the best performance that I ever gave, an Academy–Award winner, much along the lines of Brando's "I coulda been a contender" scene in *On the Waterfront.* I felt that I had reached this mogul, this man who appeared to have a tough exterior, but deep inside, possessed a heart of gold. Surely he would make some sort of concession for me and my family?

Finally, after looking blankly at me for what seemed an eternity, he held out a box and said, "Here kid, have a cigar." Then I was sent on my way. That was his gift to me for three years of indentured servitude. One lousy, stinkin' cigar! I didn't take it. (I'll bet it wasn't even Cuban.)

I was being represented by the William Morris Agency, and they brought in their top dogs to negotiate on my behalf. Abe Lastfogel, then the number one man, Norman Browkaw, his second-in-command and now Head Honcho, tried in vain to reason with Jack Warner. Then I personally brought in Gregory Bautzer, who was then the most widely known and powerful attorney in Beverly Hills. His stature was unmatched and today would be comparable only to Robert Shapiro. He dated everyone from Lana Turner to Rita Hayworth and later married actress Dana Wynter, who was under contract at Fox. Greg was also famous for wearing his sunglasses indoors at the Polo Lounge in the Beverly Hills Hotel to show a "coolness" about him. Mr. Bautzer really tried hard to get Jack Warner to renegotiate my contract for me.

The only headway made was getting Jack to up the ante to $750 a week, but I would have to sign a new seven-year contract. I had four years left on my current contract, and I wanted to get into the movies. Jack L. Warner did offer me one teenybopper flick called *Palm Springs Weekend* starring Connie Stevens. I was to be fourth-billed. Big deal! It didn't take a genius to figure out that Mr. Warner was trying to capitalize on the duo that sang "Kookie, Kookie, Lend Me Your Comb." I'm sure that somehow he would have figured out a way for the song to appear in the script.

If I sound like an ungrateful sap, it's because I was sincerely tired of playing Kookie after three years, and I wanted to move on. I lost out on *PT-109,* because with the role of Kookie, I soon found out that I was typecast. I studied long and hard trying to perfect Jack Kennedy's Boston accent. I thought I gave a very good test. I really looked and sounded the part of a young JFK. I heard through the grapevine that President Kennedy personally called from Washington to Jack Warner's office, stating, "I don't want Kookie to play me." He obviously knew me from the series, but he didn't want to be associated with my character. I really had that accent down cold. In the end, after Warren Beatty turned it down (he was John F. Kennedy's personal choice), Cliff Robertson played the president, but he did it without an accent. Go figure!

Another movie I really wanted to do was *Young Bloodhawk,* and it went to a fine actor and friend, James Franciscus.

I thought I would come out to Hollywood and become a movie star by starting with some smaller parts, working my way up to featured ones, and then graduating to starring roles. I wanted a career like Kirk Douglas, Robert Mitchum, or Burt Lancaster. The last thought in my mind was becoming a teen idol, this Kookie guy that generated the hip talk and avalanche of publicity. It was as if a tidal wave had hit me and taken me for a ride. Now, I wanted off this ride, badly.

I tried to get Efrem and Roger in on the act and take a walk with me. "Guys, now's the time. The show can't go on without us. We're the stars here. They'll have to give us more money." They didn't want to rock the boat. I can't say I blamed them.

Greg Bautzer even went down to a Palm Springs health club on the weekend to "accidentally" bump into Jack Warner in the sauna and solve the problem in a more casual atmosphere. Jack was much too smart not to realize the meeting was anything but "coincidental." The man was a walking Rock of Gibraltar.

The series was ready to head into its third season. Either I would show up for work or I'd be on suspension without pay. I stood by my principles and was put on suspension, something I *would have not done today.* I was a young actor with no business experience, and in hindsight, I know that I made a very big mistake.

Abe Lastfogel called me into his office and came up with a temporary solution. The William Morris Agency would pay me my $500-a-week salary to stay home while they ironed out my future contract. When they settled the contract, I would pay them back for the loan they floated while I was on suspension. They suggested I leave the series and stay at home.

Jack Warner had a different game plan for me. He would bring in another actor in my stead, Troy Donahue. Troy was my main competition in those days, and he gave me a good run for my money in the teen idol department. We were always friendly when we spotted each other in the mailroom, but whenever the other left, we checked with the mail clerk to see who received more fan mail. It was petty and immature, yes, but we both had healthy egos. If Mr. Warner had his way, the public would forget about Edd Byrnes. I could be replaced without much fanfare. I'd be out for good, and Mr. Warner could tear up my contract in the process, not paying me a dime.

Luckily for me, while I sat out on my five-month hiatus, fan letters came pouring in begging for me to come back to the show. It was the worst five months of my life. When there's nothing to do for the bored and privileged, it becomes very easy to reach for the bottle.

I began to drink, not heavily, but enough to pave the way to the point of no return. I mostly hung out around the house, or I would go over to the William Morris office and badger them, "What's going on? Any progress?"

I was also catching a lot of flak around town for choosing to stay at home rather than abide by my contract. Hedda Hopper called me and scolded me over the phone, "Oh, you ungrateful son-of-a-bitch! Why don't you go back to Warner and work? Jack Warner made you who you are!" To say the least, she was not very sympathetic to my plight.

One night at a party, Lucille Ball, whom I had never met in my life, came over to me and read me the riot act.

"You just can't walk out on a series!" She yelled so loudly that everyone in the place turned to see Lucy bitch out Kookie. I didn't even know this woman. I just stared at her in shock with my jaw hitting the floor. How can you win an argument against America's sweetheart?

I did, however, receive some votes of confidence. Steve McQueen sent me a telegram that read:

> Dear Edd,
>
> I respect you for what you're doing and holding your ground.
>
> Good luck,
> Steve McQueen

Steve was sympathetic to my cause because he was having problems negotiating with Four Star Television on his series, *Wanted: Dead Or Alive.*

I later bumped into Steve a few times. When he first bought his house in Brentwood called "The Castle," I followed him in my car and lo and behold, what a house! He confided to me, "I have no idea how I'm ever going to pay for this place. You'd better believe I'm not gonna be late for work one single day."

When Steve was married to Ali MacGraw, he was by then the world's number one box-office star and liked to walk around incognito. I bumped into him outside of the Cock 'n Bull Restaurant while I was window-shopping for antiques. This voice from behind me asked, "Do you own this shop, Edd?" I turned to see this guy with a full-grown mustache and beard, wearing a black sailor's cap. He looked like a hairy version of the Old Spice man.

"No, I just had lunch at the Cock 'n Bull."

The man was pleasant enough, and we struck up a casual conversation. Then his voice started to become familiar to me.

"You son-of-a-bitch! Steve?"

It was the one and only Steve McQueen, but he looked so unlike himself.

Another person who reached out to me even more than Steve McQueen was Louella Parsons. She was my biggest supporter during those five months of torture. She wrote many articles about me and called Jack Warner a couple of times on my behalf.

"Oh, Jack," she would say in soothing manner, "why don't you let Edd go back to work? Pay him what he wants."

Louella was crucial in keeping my name alive in the newspapers while I didn't work.

I also kept in touch with my friend, Joe Finn, the cop who helped support me financially over the years. I was telling him my predicament with Jack Warner. Joe was like my big brother and if anyone hurt Edd, they hurt Joe. We enjoyed a special bond. Joe did not like what he was hearing and offered to remedy the situation in his own unique way.

Joe queried, "Maybe I should fly out there and have a nice talk with Mr. Warner himself?"

"Joe, I have all of these powerful agents negotiating for me. What makes you think Jack Warner is going to listen to a New York cop?"

"You know, Eddie," Joe said with the coolest of bravado, "it's been my experience that when I put a gun to a man's head, I usually get what I want."

I had no doubt in my mind that Joe Finn would have flown to Los Angeles, found his way into Jack Warner's office, put a gun to his head, and have him tear up my contract.

I defused the situation with my insistence on letting my agents handle it, not the way Marlon Brando took care of the problem in *The Godfather.*

"Joe, I really appreciate you wanting to come to my aid, but I don't want it to be done that way."

"OK, if you change your mind, you know where to reach me."

WHEW!

The world was crashing down all around me, so I sought professional help. I needed someone to talk to and help me get over my sudden-but-very-present depression. I turned to Augusta Malkie, a metaphysician. Gussie taught the principles of positive thinking and the science of mind. We usually sat and talked while she made me this special herb tea.

As I sat in the chair, she would feed my mind with positive thoughts about how I was in control of my own destiny. These sessions lifted my depression for the moment.

For whatever reasons, I decided to see a psychiatrist, a "respectable" Beverly Hills MD, whom I'll call "Peter."

In our first session, I found it hard to open up to Peter. My past had stayed buried for so long. I was like a tough walnut, hard to crack. Once, while being interviewed on my lunch hour during the series, a reporter started asking too many questions about my past, specifically, questions about my father. I got up and walked out the door. I felt like doing the same thing to Peter. Yet, I was there to get help. He then injected me with sodium pentothol to get me to open up, but it made me very drowsy, and I almost passed out in his office.

For our next session, Peter injected me with a mysterious, but powerful, form of heroin called Dranalfa, which I didn't know at the time. The injection consisted of half speed, half heroin, and 100 percent pure ecstasy.

"This is going to loosen you up. This will make you talk," he assured me.

Peter injected the needle full of liquid into my arm, rubbed a dab of witch hazel over the puncture, and placed a Band-Aid over the shot.

Ten seconds later, I felt an incredible rush all over my body. I was tingling from head to toe, and I never felt more free in all of my life. Suddenly, the world wasn't such a bad place. Life was wonderful, and most importantly, I could talk. The chains had been broken, and I could lift this mask that inhibited me from talking about my past.

But talk was cheap when you felt this good. I was floating above the clouds for eight hours straight. Not only did I feel light in my Gucci loafers, but I discovered some wonderful side effects to the drug. When I had sex, I could be inside a woman and not climax for two hours straight. When I did have an orgasm, *it was nothing like I had ever experienced before.* My routine developed into a familiar pattern: get to Peter's office, get the shot, get a woman, and get laid.

I found myself looking forward to visits with Peter. But it wasn't for the therapy, it was most definitely for the shot. Eventually, I would have to come down, and I became even more depressed.

I knew I wasn't getting any better, but I didn't care. I was just going to get the shot. I was like a drug addict—*I was a drug addict*—going to my connection to get my fix. There was little difference between me and any junkie out on the street, except my shots were administered in a doctor's office not in an abandoned building.

Being the addictive personality that I am, my twice-a-week sessions became daily visits, weekends included. Peter had a Cadillac, and I'd meet him in a Beverly Hills parking lot on both Saturday and Sunday, while he administered my fix in the car.

I didn't think he was doing anything wrong at first. Peter was actually a very nice guy, but I don't think he knew what he was messing with. I, on the other hand, knew how powerful the drug was and how it was controlling my life.

So there it was. Television's first teen idol could now add "junkie" to his list of credits.

CHAPTER EIGHT

My Fair Lady

I CONTINUED to use Dranalfa for the next three years, and it had helped to deaden the pain while I was out of work for those five-and-a-half months.

I sought the help of another psychiatrist, not because of my addiction, but because Peter wasn't helping me emotionally. Our therapy session ended once I received the injection.

That was when I decided to see Ernest White, MD. I told Dr. White in our first session, "I've been seeing this other psychiatrist, but I'm under a lot of pressure. I don't think he's helping much." As an afterthought, I asked, "Do you think you can give me a shot of Dranalfa?"

There was a dead silence in the room.

"Dranalfa, did you say?" Ernie asked.

"Yeah, it helps me to relax," I told him.

"I can't give you a shot of that. It's against the law. That's a form of heroin," he informed me.

That's when Ernie White earned my business.

I would bite the bullet and kick Dranalfa cold turkey. I certainly sweated it out, but I was drinking white wine to come down from the drug and take off the edge. I would soon learn that one addiction replaces another.

* * * * *

The William Morris Agency suggested that I hire a publicity firm run by Helen Ferguson. Ms. Ferguson was a former actress, and her office was inside the William Morris Agency building on El Camino Drive. She was a very expensive "secretary." A telephone conversation with Helen could go on for hours if you let it. That lady was born to filibuster.

She represented almost all of the big stars in Hollywood. Her clientele included Barbara Stanwyck, Loretta Young, and Robert Taylor. Helen was very shrewd, and she was constantly getting her stars all sorts of press attention. Whenever I was interviewed, Helen would tell me to mention her other clients. For example, if I was asked "Who's your favorite actress?" I'd respond, "Barbara Stanwyck and Loretta Young." One hand washed the other.

When I was on suspension, Helen came up with the idea that I should park cars at the Sands Hotel in Las Vegas. The purpose was simple, if people recognized Edd Byrnes parking cars at the Sands, I'd get big tips and I'd earn more money parking cars than I did on a television series. If the media got wind of that, the public would really see that I was getting seriously underpaid and the backlash would force Jack L. Warner to cave in.

I actually did park cars for a day. Hell, I would do anything to break the monotony of my life at that moment. Customers of the casino would drive up, hand me their keys, and then recognize me. "Hey, it's Edd Byrnes parking my car! Oh, I get it. Great gag. Good joke!" Customers thought I was doing it for publicity.

But it was no joke. Kookie was broke.

A parking lot–attendant union official had heard of my publicity stunt and ordered me to stop. Damn, they had a union for everything in that town! I was actually relieved. To go from being a television star who played a parking lot attendant to *actually* parking cars for a living is a little like switching your diet from filet mignon to Spam. There's just no comparison.

Asa was tiring of me and my noncommittal, philandering ways. We had been dating for five years. During the last year, she was living with me in my house on Bowmont Drive off Coldwater Canyon. She had known of my affairs but wanted a commitment from me. Asa had reached the end of her rope, and now I was under the gun. "Marry me or I'm history," was pretty much the message.

My typical male response was, "Well, give me two weeks to think about it."

I truly did love Asa, but one problem remained: *I STILL WANTED IT ALL!!!* I was a major television star, twenty-seven years old, and I wanted to sow my wild oats. Asa, I knew, loved me unconditionally, and she wasn't a "Johnny Come Lately." She loved me way before I became famous.

Another reason I didn't want to marry Asa was that she had a *weird* family. I knew I was not only going to be married to Asa, but I was going to be married to her family as well.

Her father was an alcoholic, and her mother was a typical mother-in-law. In addition, she had two sisters that I liked, but they were just a tad bit distant. That made it four out of four relatives who were not what I considered "normal." It was a perfect batting average.

Asa did give me that two weeks to think things over. I decided that I would fly to Europe, sleep with as many women as I could, and if that didn't change my mind, then I would marry Asa. Now, I'll bet you feminists out there are frothing at the mouth right at this point. I was an immature kid who was stuck in a situation that I didn't want to be in. I felt as if Asa, instead of Joe Finn, was holding a gun to my head and forcing me to make a decision. I can't fault Asa for that, but I wanted to have my cake and eat it, too.

I flew to Paris, keeping company with a woman in the Lancaster Hotel. The funny thing about this hotel was that unless you had a sitting room for a lady, you weren't allowed to have a member of the opposite sex in the room. I had a regular room sans the sitting room. I went out on a date that first night. My lady friend and I were in the lobby, heading up to my room, when I was politely informed at the front desk of their policy.

"What do you mean I can't take a woman up to my room?"

"Monsieur, you do not have a sitting room in your suite; therefore, she cannot accompany you to your room."

My temper flared, and I fired back, "This is Paris, France! You people *fuck* at the drop of a hat!" As an afterthought, I gritted my teeth and growled, "And besides, I plan to have sex with the lady in the bedroom, not in the sitting room."

He didn't take kindly to my remarks, so I checked out of the hotel and into another.

I then headed to Cannes, the wonderful south of France, the playground for the rich and the beautiful. I stayed at the Carlton Hotel. The minute I checked in, a woman's voice called out, "Eddie?"

I didn't know her, but she was very attractive. She was my companion for the rest of my stay there. In Monaco, my new friend and I were running out of money, so I telephoned my parental substitutes, Warner Brothers.

"Hugh Benson's office, please."

"Yeah, Edd," Hugh answered.

"I'm in Monaco and I'm down to my last couple of francs. Would you have the studio wire me two thousand dollars?"

Hugh replied, "Sounds like you're living like a movie star."

Warner did wire me the money in spite of our contract dispute. That basically ended our unpleasantness and put our relationship back on the right foot. I decided then and there to go back to the series and finish up the commitment on my seven-year contract.

After my wild time in England and France, I returned to Los Angeles prepared to work and marry Asa. I was looking forward to a wild bachelor party to send me off in the right direction.

Efrem and Roger were at the party along with almost everyone else from the show. Solly Buyono brought some strippers, and we played a classic gag on Efrem. The party was held at Roger's house, and when the doorbell rang, Roger said, "Efrem, could you get the door, please? I've got to get something in the back room." Anyone who knows Efrem knows that he is the ultimate gentleman, and what you see on screen is what you get in real life. Efrem is also a very religious man, but he is not pious. He is perfectly capable of having a good time with anyone. Efrem opened the door to find a beautiful brunette wearing high heels and a fur coat.

Efrem almost bit through his pipe, "Mmmm, yes, dear?"

"Hi, Mr. Zimbalist. Is this the bachelor party for Edd Byrnes?"

"Yes, my dear, you've come to the right place. Please, won't you come in?"

"You're so kind, Mr. Zimbalist. Would you please take my coat?"

"Yes, my dear, I would be most happy to."

She took off her coat, and she wasn't wearing a stitch of clothing. I didn't watch her, I was looking for some kind of expression on Efrem's face, any sign of lecherous behavior to see if there was a dual personality behind that polite exterior. He played it very cool. "Oh, yes my dear, very nice," was his response to this stark-naked beauty. I was gravely disappointed by his reaction.

The rest of the night was a blur of debauchery, but I do remember naked girls running around the house, getting smashed, swimming in the pool, alcohol flowing like the Mississippi River. Everyone left that night with a smile on their face, only to be replaced by a hangover in the morning. Just what your basic All-American bachelor party should be.

Jack Entrotter, the owner of the Sands in Las Vegas, offered to pay for our wedding, and everyone's plane ticket if we would have the ceremony at the Sands. I guess he figured it would be great publicity for the hotel.

I said thanks, but no thanks. "Why not?" he pressed for an answer.

"Jack, that's very generous, but everyone I know who gets married in Las Vegas ends up getting a divorce."

Jack had a good laugh, but had a zinger of his own, "That's funny, Edd, everyone I know who gets married in Beverly Hills ends up getting a divorce." The man had a point.

On my wedding day, I remember playing over and over again the song, "Get Me to the Church on Time," from the *My Fair Lady* soundtrack. Roger Smith was my best man, and he was supposed to pick me up and take me to the church in Beverly Hills. We had some champagne, and then Roger decided he wanted to get his car washed. I objected, "Roger, we can't get to the church late."

My best man said, "We can't show up to the church and the reception in a dirty car." It sort of made sense to me at the time, but we didn't realize how many car washes were closed on Sunday. We arrived at the church a half-hour late. It put everyone a little bit on edge, knowing my reluctance to get married in the first place. I imagine Asa thought for at least thirty minutes that she was going to be left at the altar. That song must have been a bad omen.

Asa and I made our marriage official on March 6, 1962. We had a beautiful ceremony in a Beverly Hills church and held our reception at our favorite restaurant, La Scala, with sixty or so of our closest friends. As a wedding present, I bought my new bride a string of white pearls and later a red Mercedes 190 SL convertible. We were young, beautiful, wealthy, with a nice Beverly Hills home complete with a wine cellar built by Roger Smith.

I had everything any man could want, but it was not enough. There was a hole inside of me, and it constantly needed to be filled. I had it all, but I didn't feel I deserved any of it, so I went out of the way to sabotage my life, not caring whom I hurt in the process. Especially Asa.

* * * * *

After five months of intense negotiating with Jack Warner, the William Morris Agency finally came to an agreement with the mogul. My contract salary was to be the same, but I was entitled to 50 percent of any of my promotional appearances I made on behalf of the show. That was it. That's why I sat around on my duff doing nothing for five months going crazy?

Jack Warner also offered me my own television series, if I would sign another seven-year contract, but I was not about to shoot myself in the foot again. Feeling rebuffed, Jack Warner made sure I never made a movie for him ever again. And I never did.

I returned to *77 Sunset Strip* as a newer, cleaned-up version of Kookie. I figured that the character had grown older and couldn't keep parking cars forever, so the jive talk and the jacket were replaced with a suit and tie. I became a partner in the agency and was now seen as an equal, not a kid who spouted out nonsensical words.

In hindsight, it wasn't such a good idea. At the end of the fourth year, when I left, the show still had a respectable 25.8 share in the Nielsens and was ranked the thirteenth highest television series overall.

When I returned to the series as a cleaned-up, respectable, user-friendly Kookie, the ratings plummeted and never returned to its once-hallowed popularity.

Though my part became much bigger and juicier, the show became a grind. My heart was no longer in it, and I was counting the days until my contract ran out.

What made the time go by much slower was the fact that Roger Smith ended up leaving. Roger had tripped down a flight of stairs in his own house while carrying a hi-fi stereo. He often came to work complaining of headaches and was downing lots of aspirin.

I'd tell him, "Roger, you need to see a doctor."

He finally did. He was x-rayed, and the doctor found a blood clot in his head. He went into surgery immediately, and they had to perform major surgery to remove the clot. Roger was out for more than a year, but that wasn't the worst of it. He had to learn how to speak all over again. My good friend with whom I shared so many good times was now gone for an undetermined amount of time. Efrem stayed on, but it just wasn't the same without Roger.

By 1963, the novelty of the show had worn thin and was in serious decline. In an attempt to save it, actor Jack Webb of *Dragnet* fame was brought in as the producer. Jack let it be known in no uncertain terms that drastic changes were going to be made.

The first thing Jack did was to hire his friend and fellow actor, William Conrad, as director. I soon had a falling out with Conrad over his dictatorial style on the set. Former actors usually make the best directors because they can appreciate the actor and know how to communicate with them. Conrad was the exception.

Practically the first thing Conrad said to me was "Now, Edd, this is how I think Kookie would react to this."

"Wait a minute," I objected. "I've been playing this character for five years, and you start telling me how he thinks?"

Who did this clown think he was, telling me how my character thinks and reacts? All of a sudden, he's giving me acting advice. He became verbally abusive, criticizing and putting me down.

I refused to work with Conrad until he apologized. I stormed off to my dressing room, mad and upset. He was definitely the fat man, but I was no Jake. We had a major falling out, and Hugh Benson and our other producers, Howie Horowitz and Bill Orr, had to come to my dressing room to smooth things over. They asked me what the problem was.

My response was direct and to the point: "I'll tell you the problem, William Conrad's a bully. Tell that asshole not to tell me how to play a part that I've done successfully for five fucking years!" Yes, you might say that I was angry. Conrad did come to my dressing room to apologize, but our relationship was never considered "warm."

The only good thing about the dispute was that Jack Webb came to appreciate the depths of my unhappiness and agreed to let me out of my contract with Warner Brothers nine months early to do a movie for United Artists called *The Secret Invasion.* For that, I'll be eternally grateful to Jack Webb. By the end of 1963, I had done my time at Warner Brothers, and I was a free man.

With Roger and me gone, Efrem was left to fend for himself. Efrem's character, Bailey, was transformed into an international operative and filmed several episodes on the road. The new format didn't work with the audience. The show had been dealt a death blow. ABC-TV and Warner Brothers had milked the series for all its worth. The final telecast of *77 Sunset Strip* took place on September 9, 1964, almost six years after we first went on the air. The series produced 154 black-and-white episodes running until the end of the 1964 season. The show was in syndication from 1966 until 1990, a great success in anyone's book. It became a part of television history.

* * * * *

I was relieved of the daily grind of the series, but then I discovered, if I didn't work, I didn't get paid. My lifestyle had been extravagant ever since I met John Harjes, and it accelerated when I made it in Hollywood. It's so easy to get accustomed to a certain way of life, but then the carpet gets pulled out from under you.

In addition to high mortgage and car payments, psychiatrists' fees (Asa was seeing one as well), I was still supporting my mother and sister in New York. Asa and I flew to New York to cut the umbilical cord in person and tell them the well had run dry. They did not take the news well. I paid their rent for five years and explained that

I could no longer carry them, what with the series, the new house, the foreign cars, the wife, and so on.

As it turned out, it was the best thing that ever happened to them. My mother and Jo-Ann moved to Los Angeles to be closer to me. In addition, my mother met a nice man and got married again.

* * * * *

I was seeing Ernie White in therapy, but still I found myself quite unhappy. Ernie tried to help as much as he could, but he just wasn't that experienced. I saw him over a period of five years and estimated that I must have paid him close to thirty-five-thousand dollars.

I left Ernie White a dejected and torn man. I ran into him a few years later at Heathrow Airport in London. He had now grown a full beard and sported long hair. He looked like a hippie who was trying to find himself, yet he was putting on the facade of a man who had it all together.

I was resentful, and I told him, "You know, Ernie, you did not help me at all. The money I gave you, the thirty-five-thousand-dollars worth of business, I should have just flushed down the toilet. At least then, I would have known exactly where the money was going."

He was taken aback and even sounded like a psychiatrist when he apologized, "I'm sorry you feel that way, Edd, but I thank you for your honesty."

If he wanted honesty, he was going to get more of it and then some. I didn't let up, "You were a total failure in my life, Ernie. I just wanted you to know that."

I didn't know what I was looking for, maybe a father figure. Ernie was a few years older than I was, and I thought he might have the answers for me. Unfortunately, he didn't.

In despair, my answers would temporarily come in a bottle, that liquid form of mass destruction we call alcohol.

CHAPTER NINE

European Vacation

IN HOLLYWOOD, when you're hot you're hot, and when you're not, you're not. By 1963, my career had seriously cooled down.

The $250,000 movie offers were no longer rolling in. I had stayed with *77 Sunset Strip* two years longer than I should have. If I had left the show at the height of my popularity, I would not have been in this current predicament.

Roger Corman, an independent filmmaker, wanted me for his next picture, *The Secret Invasion.*

If you know anything about the picture-making business, you know that Roger Corman is known as the "King of the B-movies." The budget for a Corman picture isn't exactly champagne and caviar. You would be lucky to get Brown Derby beer and stale crackers, but that didn't mean I wasn't grateful to be working. United Artists was distributing the film, and it was the highest budgeted film of Corman's "bargain basement" career.

The William Morris Agency had received a call from Roger Corman to see if I might be interested in doing a movie for him in Yugoslavia.

"Well, who's going to be in the picture?" I asked.

"They've got Stewart Granger, Mickey Rooney, Raf Vallone, and Bobby Darin." Darin had just finished *Hell Is for Heroes* and was a hot new star.

"They've got Raf Vallone signed?" I was intrigued to be working with Granger and Rooney, but the thought of working with Raf Vallone excited me. He's a wonderful character actor and is considered an icon in Italy.

I was sent the script and actually liked it, though my character was killed off three-quarters of the way into the picture.

The Secret Invasion was also the first film where I was actually billed as "Edd Byrnes." In the past, I had been billed as "Edward Byrnes." For some reason, I just didn't like the sound of it. There was nothing unusual about the name, and it didn't look good in print. The fan magazines had been spelling "Edd" with two Ds. I remembered my good friend from New York, Edd Kramer, who spelled his first name with two D's. Ah, yes, that was much better and unusual. Ever since then, it's been "Edd." Incidentally, Edd Kramer was thirty-five years old when he got drunk one night and went to bed with a lit cigarette in his hand. He burned himself to death, as did another good friend of mine, Jack Cassidy.

Roger Corman, Asa, and I took the same flight to Rome and then later to Yugoslavia. Roger had his nose deep into a book and had two others sitting on his lap. I looked over, and all three books were on "How to Direct Movies." *Oh my God!* I thought. *He's reading books on how to direct. Am I in trouble or what?*

When we got to Dubrovnik, Yugoslavia, we discovered it was a walled-in fifteenth-century fort that the Slavs had built to keep out the Turks. It was a beautiful and quaint little city. We also discovered the conditions in Dubrovnik were not just a few years behind the times. It was very primitive in an unusual sort of way.

Asa and I checked into a hotel, complete with a marvelous view of the Adriatic. It cost five dollars a night, but even at that rate, we were being overcharged for the hotel's services. I had to wake up early in the mornings for our shooting schedule, and often had to shave by candlelight with a straight razor and cold running water.

Stewart Granger, Mickey Rooney, and Raf Vallone had it much easier. They had rented their own villas, while Asa and I preferred to stay in this hotel.

Stewart Granger liked to be called "Jim." His real name was James Stewart, but of course, another famous actor held claim to that name so he changed his first name to Stewart.

Stewart had it a little better than any of us. He was fifty-two and had a twenty-two-year-old French actress staying with him at the villa. She was devastatingly beautiful. Stewart never let her leave the house. She would stay there and sunbathe in the nude all day. When he came home from the shoot, she would serve him a drink and have dinner waiting for him. You could say he wasn't really roughing it in Yugoslavia.

Mickey Rooney was the very first movie star from whom I had gotten an autograph. It was when I was fourteen and playing hooky from school. I was hanging out in Central Park, pretending I was Tarzan when I recognized this little man. I went up to him and timidly asked, "Mr. Rooney, can I have your autograph?"

"Sure kid," and he just wrote, "Mickey Rooney." Little did I know that fifteen years later I would be starring in a movie with him.

Mickey was drinking heavily in those days, and he was a wild man. He'd always try to improvise his scenes. He'd take a look at the script and tear up the pages, but he was a major talent. He could do anything on camera, and it was nice to work with a legend. Mickey also had his food flown in from Rome because he couldn't stand the food in Yugoslavia. Mickey would always say, "If I can't pronounce it, I sure as hell ain't gonna eat it!" It was fun working with Mickey, and I learned a lot from him.

During the middle of filming, Mickey's wife, actress Barbara Ann Thomason, was murdered in their Beverly Hills home by Milos Milocevic, an aspiring actor from Belgrade. Milos and Barbara had been having an affair, and Barbara had decided to end it. Milos broke in, and they ended up shooting each other. Milocevic's body was found slumped over Barbara Thomason's. She used Mickey's .38 revolver to kill him. Everyone on the set in Dubrovnik was shocked. We didn't know what to say or do to comfort our costar. It was tragic. To this day, Mickey claims, "What happened to her is the saddest part of my life."

I struck up a friendship with Raf Vallone that remains strong to this day. We took a liking to each other, but Raf was having serious problems with the English language. This was one of his first English-speaking roles, and I guess I was the only one he felt comfortable enough to come up to and ask, "Edduh, howa you pronounce-ah that-ah word-ah?" He had to learn his lines phonetically. If you watch him in the movie, you'll notice the language wasn't coming easy to him, but I certainly couldn't fault him for that. My Italian is quite-ah bad-ah.

Raf and I had many adventures when the movie was over. He came back to California to work in *Nevada Smith*, starring Steve McQueen. He rented a penthouse in Westwood, and I showed him a good time while in Los Angeles.

Once we went to the Beverly Hills Hotel and ran into agent Kurt Frings having lunch poolside with two gorgeous girls. One was a Polish actress, and the other was a photographer/model from London. Both were in their early twenties. Somehow, we managed to lure them away from Kurt. We drove to a Malibu beach house that was loaned out by the studio to Raf on weekends. Later I learned that Kurt was furious with me.

We arrived at the beach house on a Friday and didn't leave until Monday. We partied and drank; Raf cooked pasta, and we danced and made love. You name the hedonistic act, we did it.

Raf was a lover of life. He loved to eat, he loved to cook, he loved to work, and he *especially* loved women. That weekend, he gravitated to the Polish lady, and I ended up with the English model. Later at my suggestion, the two women joined him in bed, and I walked in on them after they had made love. Raf, basking in the afterglow, was sitting up with his arms around both girls.

"Edduh, this is-ah the first time-ah I've ever made love with two girls at-ah one time-ah. It's just maw-velous! Just maw-velous!"

I found it ironic that in *Nevada Smith*, Raf played a priest who tried to teach Steve McQueen to give up his life of sin. Obviously, Raf was not a method actor.

When I went to visit Raf and his family in Sperlonga, Italy, halfway between Naples and Rome, I discovered Raf had two lovely, exotic-looking daughters, aged sixteen and eighteen. His eighteen-year-old had eyes for me, and her perceptive father picked up on our mutual attraction. When Raf was out of earshot, I whispered to her, "Now, when Raf goes to bed, I'll sneak down to your bedroom."

The Italian actor was no dummy. He knew me too well, knew how much I loved the opposite sex, and wasn't going to let me touch one single hair on her precious little head despite our friendship. This was daddy's little girl, and she was off limits to Edduh.

In Italy, most of the homes have bars on the windows because they have a major problem with burglary. Raf not only had bars on the windows of the villa but had a barbed-wire fence surrounding the entire compound. It was his own little Alcatraz, and Raf was the warden.

Not only was this house locked up tighter than a drum, but the doors on his daughters' rooms had reverse locks on them. Once his daughters went to bed, he locked them in their rooms for the night. Each had a bathroom, but they couldn't get out until the morning until Warden Raf unlocked their cells.

When I thought that Raf was asleep, I quietly crept over, like an escaped convict in tennis shoes, to their bedrooms and discovered the reverse locks. I quickly went to plan B. I opened my door, dropped down from the balcony, and tried to slip in through the bedroom window, but then I discovered the metal bars that separated *me* from *her.* Plan C was to give it up, spank the monkey, go to bed, and toss and turn. I'm sure Raf slept like a baby that night, chuckling himself to sleep knowing his daughters were locked up like the gold in Fort Knox. Thanks, Raf, for a sleepless night in your villa.

Working with Stewart Granger, I discovered, was going to be a tumultuous experience. He was a volatile guy with both a sweet and nasty disposition. Sober, he was nice as could be. When he drank though, the dark side of his personality would come out. He'd snap at Roger Corman, "Give me my fifteen thousand dollars in expense money now or I'm leaving this godforsaken place!" He could get downright ornery.

I also discovered that Stewart had a bad habit of changing other actors' dialogue for the benefit of himself. Henry Silva, another actor in the movie, had had his lines changed by Stewart, so I knew what lay ahead for me. Stewart tried to pull the same stunt when the time came for our big scene together. I came on the set, and while rehearsing, Stewart butted in and said, "Oh no, Edd, you're not going to say that speech."

"What are you talking about?" I asked anxiously.

"You're not going to do that speech."

"Stewart, you're cutting out all of my lines," I objected. "This is a good scene. One of the reasons why I wanted to do this picture was because of this scene."

The scene took place in a hotel room, and I had to confront Stewart one-on-one. He didn't want his character to appear weak, so he tried to weaken mine. It was a game of one-upsmanship on his part. If another actor had a great line, he had to have one greater, *and* the last line.

Roger Corman had no control over Stewart whatsoever. I knew that if I even so much as blinked, Stewart would be all over me. Luckily, he backed down, but I could tell he was still sulking and wouldn't speak to me for a few days. I decided to make the first move, so when I saw him sitting in the corner, I went over to him and put my arm around him and said, "Jimmy, you know, another reason I wanted to do this movie was I wanted to work with you. That's the truth." That got him out of his funk, and we finished the picture without any more confrontations. I liked him a lot, but he sure was one moody bastard. Nevertheless, he was a great host, storyteller, and bartender.

I was in Yugoslavia for seven weeks, and all throughout the filming, everyone in the cast and crew drank. I discovered that in Yugoslavia, drinking is a way of life. Alcohol, in all its forms, is everywhere you go throughout Europe. For lunch, especially in Italy or Spain, there's always a large bottle of white or red wine to drink with your meal. Here in the States, they frown upon drinking that early, but over there, it's the norm. I didn't drink much during the picture, but off the set it became a bigger part of my life.

From Dubrovnik, I went to Munich, Germany, to appear in a variety show. The producers had flown to Dubrovnik to close the deal with me. While in Munich, I received an offer I couldn't refuse. I performed in a nightclub in Berlin. I was still a very big star in Germany and had been offered several films, but I never took them up on it.

Because Asa and I rented out our home to Roger Smith, who was now married to Ann-Margret, I often stayed in Natalie Wood's guest room in Brentwood when back in the States. Natalie surrounded herself with an inner circle of friends and confidants. She employed two men at the time, Mart Crowley and Howard Jeffries. They were both known homosexuals, and she always felt safe with them.

Natalie and R. J. had always been very generous and giving. R. J. used to give Mart all of his tailor-made shirts when he no longer wanted them. It was comical that Mart would want to wear them since each one had "R. J." stitched on the pocket. The shirts also would hang off Mart because he wasn't as well built as R. J.

Natalie fed these guys, gave them money, and encouraged them to be something other than her personal secretary. Mart Crowley wrote *The Boys in the Band,* which was a successful Broadway play that was made into a movie and directed by the talented William Friedkin.

During one stay with the Wagners, I woke up in the middle of the night because I felt someone's presence in the room. When I looked up, there was just a bit of light shining in the room, and I saw Mart Crowley staring down at me from the bedside. He scared the shit out of me.

"WHAT THE FUCK ARE YOU DOING?" I screamed and pushed him away.

He said softly, "I couldn't sleep, so I just wanted to come down and look at you. You're so beautiful."

He didn't flatter me, and I didn't let up, "Get the fuck out of here. What the hell is wrong with you?"

We've run into each other since then, and I've made amends to Mart about that night, but he truly scared me. He told me he was drunk and wandering around in a daze.

On that same trip, I was asked by Bob Hope to join him for his variety special "Bob Hope Presents The Chrysler Theatre" at Universal.

For some strange reason, Bob has always been very nice to me. He remembers who I am and never fails to recognize me. A few years later, his people asked me to emcee one of his shows with Vikki Carr opening in North Carolina.

I went backstage to Bob's dressing room where he thanked me profusely. "Is there any special way you would like for me to introduce you to the audience, Bob?" I asked.

He told me how to say word for word the special introduction, and it was a done deal. I first introduced Vikki Carr to the crowd, and she performed for nearly forty-five minutes. I went back to my dressing room, opened up a bottle of white wine, and started talking to some people in the show. The next thing I knew, Bob Hope was up on stage and into his act. I had completely forgotten to introduce this legend.

His producer asked me in typical Hollywood fashion, "Edd, baby, what happened to you?"

I asked, "Wasn't somebody supposed to come and tell me when Bob was ready? Where was my cue?" I laugh now, but it was terribly embarrassing for me then, but I was busy drinking.

About ten years ago, I was in Las Vegas with a friend. Bob Hope was in town performing on the Strip. My friend wanted to see him, so we went and were seated in a booth. It was almost a repeat performance of the night Elvis introduced me to the audience. Bob did the same thing, and I was deeply touched, even more so than when Elvis did it. I was even more impressed that a man in his eighties could get up and perform for ninety minutes, entertain people, and make them laugh. He's a great entertainer and has a much better memory than I can ever expect to possess.

I also met Sal Mineo on that Bob Hope variety special, and we developed a friendship over the years. I was one of the last people to see Sal alive before he was killed in a robbery.

I was in the Cock 'n Bull when he came over to my table and invited me to the opening of his new play, *P.S. Your Cat Is Dead*, the next night in Westwood. I planned to go. The next morning, I had a tennis match with a friend. I lived in Marina Del Rey at the time and had an apartment with a balcony overlooking the tennis court. My friend yelled up at me from below, "Hey Edd, did you hear what happened to Sal Mineo last night?"

My heart stopped, and I braced myself for what was to come next. I replied cautiously, "No, I didn't hear. What happened?"

"He was stabbed to death in his garage."

I couldn't believe it. I was grief stricken. Sal was one of the sweetest guys I had ever known, and he was a very talented actor.

I told my friend that I had a drink with him just that night before and how it was so strange that someone can die within the blink of an eye.

Two weeks after Sal's death, a couple of Los Angeles police detectives came to see me. I opened the door, and one of them said, "We heard you were one of the last few people to see Sal Mineo alive."

"That's right. I was wondering when you were going to show up." I repeated the story to them, for whatever it was worth. The case was to take a strange twist. A convict bragged to another man in jail that he was the one that killed the famous Sal Mineo. The convict was brought up on charges. He later proved in court that he was just bragging and was not the killer. Poor Sal was only thirty-seven when he was taken from us.

* * * * *

Beach Ball was a typical mindless beach movie in the spirit of Frankie Avalon and Annette Funicello. I was continually offered this type of film after I was released from my contract at Warner Brothers. However, the producers of *Beach Ball* were going to give me so much money, it would have been ridiculous to turn down Paramount's generous offer. Beach pictures often came with a stigma, and I vowed to only do it this one time, not wanting to become another Frankie Avalon.

I must admit, the picture was a romp, and I couldn't complain about the ideal surroundings at a Malibu location, girls in bikinis as far as the eye could see and great weather. The Beach Boys couldn't have had it any better!

The movie also featured Diana Ross and the Supremes in a cameo appearance. I used to talk with them between takes. They were all very young, nice girls. I was extremely happy for the meteoric rise in their careers.

Because of my vow not to do another beach picture, I found myself constantly unemployed. My, how your fortune can change in Hollywood overnight. Just a few years earlier, I was the cock of the walk. Now, I was just a feather duster.

If I wasn't drowning my sorrows in white wine, I was trying to think of ways to get work. Either way, drunk or hung over, my head wasn't very clear.

It was Asa who thought of going to Europe and looking for work. *77 Sunset Strip* was enormously popular there, and based upon my popularity, I'd surely get job offers. Then she got even more specific, "What about Italy, Edd? Clint Eastwood made it big over there in the spaghetti Westerns, and as a result, he became a star in the States."

Asa always had a good head for business, and I thought it was a fantastic idea, but we certainly weren't going to be offered the films on a silver platter. I had to make the tough decision to live in Rome, get an agent, then hope I would get some work.

So it was that we decided to go to Rome and look for work. Asa would audition for parts, as well, and as luck would have it, it was our saving grace.

That's when we rented our house out to Roger Smith and Ann-Margret. After packing up our belongings, we headed for Europe.

In Rome, we found a great apartment and hired a cook since we both would be looking for work. One of our neighbors was Zoe Sallis, an actress who had a son, Danny, with director John Huston. I'd see John visiting Zoe and Danny a lot and had the opportunity to get to know him. Danny was just a kid when I'd go over to their apartment and play with him. He has since followed in his famous father's footsteps and has become a director as well.

Jack Palance was another actor that I would run into quite a bit while in Rome. He's a nice guy, but surprisingly very quiet. I had once set him up on a date with Zoe Sallis, and Jack brought along his daughter, Holly. Jack was paying more attention to his daughter than Zoe. Toward the end of the meal, Zoe got up and asked me to escort her to the bathroom.

"Edd, what's the matter with Jack? He won't talk to me. I'm getting out of here. I've never met anybody so rude." She left in a huff.

When I went back to the table, I had a chance to talk to Jack alone.

"Where's Zoe?" Jack asked.

"She left, Jack. She really liked you but wanted to know why you didn't pay much attention to her."

Jack's response amused me, "When I'm with my daughter, Holly, I don't pay much attention to other women."

My auspicious European film career got underway when my agent, Gino Malare, sent both Asa and me to see Italian movie producer Enzio Gerolomi. Enzio was a well-known producer and employed his two sons in the film business, one as a director and the other as an actor.

Asa and I had a meeting with Enzio, but they were held separately. I met with him first, we talked, but he didn't commit himself one way or the other. I could tell he hadn't made up his mind when I left. There was no firm offer.

I went downstairs and found Asa waiting in our new car. It was a gift from a German producer who wanted me to do a movie, but had no start date yet. Would I keep myself available to him? He was never able to raise the money. The car had been picked up in Germany, and it was a welcome gift.

Asa asked, "So, how did it go?"

"I don't know. He didn't make an offer. Let's just say he wasn't cuckoo for Kookie."

It was now Asa's turn to be interviewed. Enzio didn't know that Asa and I were married because she still went by her maiden name when she got acting parts. He knew her as "Asa Maynor," not "Mrs. Edd Byrnes."

Knowing her husband was not offered the part and feeling a bit uncertain, Asa made small talk by asking Enzio who was going to be in his movie.

"Gilbert Roland-ah, and maybe another American actor named Edduh Byrnes-ah."

Asa asked quizzically, "Did you say Edd Byrnes?"

"Yeah, you know, Edduh Brynes-ah, the American actor from-ah *77 Sunset Strip*?"

"Edd Byrnes . . . " she said, still acting puzzled, "that's . . . that's impossible. No, no, no. Edd Byrnes is much too expensive. You can't get him. He's a huge star all over the world. You couldn't possibly have him signed to your film. Do you have that kind of budget?"

Now, the producer was deeply offended, and his Italian ego surfaced. He had to have Edduh Byrnes-ah in his movie. "Oh yeah, no problem. Edd's-uh gonna do our-ah movie."

Suddenly, he was turned on to the idea of starring me in his picture because Asa was hyping me till kingdom come.

Enzio Gerolomi ended up calling my agent, telling him he wanted me ever so badly. I got a thirty-five-thousand-dollar offer to do his picture, along with three others when I was finished with this film.

All of this *and* top billing over Gilbert Roland! I owed it all to my beautiful, if somewhat cunning, wife. Enzio did get his money's worth. I performed all of my own stunts, and there were *a lot* of them.

Speaking of Gilbert Roland, I found him to be a top-notch gentleman. We had one scene together where we were both riding on horseback going down a slope. I was in front and when I looked back, he had fallen off his horse and was rolling down the hill. At that time, he must have been in his early seventies, but he was in great shape even then. He got back on his horse and continued on with the scene. Gilbert started each morning of his life by doing 200 sit-ups and 100 push-ups. He had a thirty-inch waist his whole life.

In Spain, Gilbert was considered a real hero and invited me to the best restaurants where we were treated like royalty. He was also a bullfight aficionado, and we once got into a conversation about the sport. He felt that bullfighting was an art, but I told him it was a cruel sport because the bull rarely, if ever, wins. Despite that one "flaw," Gilbert was a wonderful human being and a great movie star, which he so aptly played in *The Bad and the Beautiful.*

We had stayed in Europe for more than a year when I decided it was time to get back to the States. I did three films back-to-back and made quite a bit of money. So did Enzio's movies. A year was more than enough time away from the States, and I didn't want to be forgotten in my own country. So we moved back to our comfortable Beverly Hills home. I knew in the back of my mind that the movie-going public was very fickle. I was afraid that people might say one day, "Edd who?" Fame is so fleeting.

I didn't want to be another casualty of the industry. Hollywood was a place with a longstanding tradition of high turnover and very short memory.

CHAPTER TEN

My Cheatin' Heart

THE MONEY I had saved in Italy was burning a hole in my pocket. I was being paid weekly in lire, and it didn't cost much to live there, so I saved any cash I made in a safety deposit box.

When I returned to our home on Hutton Drive in Benedict Canyon, I went out and bought a Rolls-Royce but not without first getting Cary Grant's approval.

I met Cary Grant in Jack Warner's private dining room and was thrilled to get the chance to know him. He was the consummate movie star.

During the midsixties, I tried to produce a script that I had in my possession. I sent that script to Cary Grant, thinking he'd be perfect for it.

Returning home from work a few days later, I asked Asa if anyone had called for me.

"Yeah, someone trying to impersonate Cary Grant," my wife informed me, and then as an afterthought, she started to laugh.

I hadn't told Asa about sending the script. Now I said seriously, "That probably was Cary Grant."

"Why would Cary Grant be calling you?" she asked.

"I sent him a script that I wanted him to do."

I called Cary back, and he said he had just completed filming *Charade* with Audrey Hepburn, and the script I had sent him was almost identical.

He then added, "Edd, that wife of yours, she giggled throughout our entire conversation. Is she all right?"

"To be honest, Cary, she thought it was someone else doing a bad impersonation of you," I laughed.

The icon replied in a serious tone, "Oh yes, yes. I get that all the time."

When Asa and I returned from Italy, Cary invited me over for dinner. After the meal, we went outside on the patio. I said to the revered statesman of film, "Cary, I'm thinking of buying a Rolls-Royce. The only problem is, I feel that I'm much too young to own that type of a car. I don't want to drive around Beverly Hills in a Rolls-Royce and have people thinking I'm a snob."

Mr. Grant's tone was adamant. "Edd, if you want a Rolls-Royce, just go out and buy it. You deezuv it," and that ended that. His finality was all I needed to hear.

I drove out to Pasadena with a friend of mine the next day and paid for the 1962 black 19 Silver Cloud in hard, cold cash. I had not mentioned the idea of buying this luxurious car to my beloved spouse. So when I drove the car up to the house with hopes of surprising her with my new toy, she was furious. Perhaps even outraged.

Asa was the practical one in our marriage. If I wanted to buy a three-thousand-dollar antique, Asa would prefer to put the three thousand dollars in our savings account.

Natalie Wood introduced me to her business manager, Andrew Marie, Jr., of the Andrew Morgan Marie Company. In addition to

Natalie, he managed Humphrey Bogart's, Dick Powell's, and June Allyson's money. He possessed a brilliant and creative mind regarding finances, and when he retired, he left the business to his son, Andrew Marie III.

I felt that his son was less than good for me. Natalie once called him and said, "I don't have a car. What's the most economical thing to do?" His answer: "Go to Hertz and rent one." That was typical of his attitude. He never went out of his way to get special deals for his clients as far as I know. He would prefer to ride his motorcycle than to take care of his clients' financial matters.

Andy III put me on a savings plan that ended in disaster. His plan was to put me on a fifty-dollar-a-week allowance for walking-around money. Now, I could sign my name at any restaurant in Beverly Hills and have the bill sent to Andy. I would, on average, go out to restaurants (Cock 'n Bull, Scandia, Chasens, La Scala, and the Polo Lounge) about five times a week and just sign my name to the check. At the end of the month, I'd get these astronomical bills from the restaurants ranging from $800 to a $1,000 or more—all in a single month.

Foolishly, I thought I was saving huge amounts of money by having only fifty dollars in my wallet, but of course, I wasn't saving a dime. Andy received a handsome 5 percent of my salary for his supposed brilliance. I got rid of Andy III and, eventually, so did Natalie.

To be quite honest, I never had a thought for tomorrow regarding money. I had it in my head that if things ever got really bad, I could always earn three thousand dollars a week. At the time, I was performing in plays in the States and Canada when I wasn't appearing in a film. My standard fee ranged from three thousand to thirty-five hundred dollars a week. Money would be another vice I'd have to get control of later in my life.

* * * * *

The midsixties had kicked in, and it was the beginning of the "free love" movement. Edd Byrnes welcomed it with open arms and a world-class grin. There was not a better place for this concept than good ol' Hollywood. Even though I was a married man, now with a child on the way, my sexual drive was revving at "full throttle."

Those sexually permissive times remind me of an incident I had at a dinner party held at Jack Cassidy's home in Bel Air. Jack was married to actress Shirley Jones. Jack and Shirley hosted a buffet with cocktails, and Jack was doing his number. Though quite the host, he, like Sammy Davis, Jr., was always "on."

Actress Linda Christian was there, as well. Linda was Tyrone Power's widow and had lost none of her radiant beauty after his death. She had these big brown eyes, silky brown hair, smooth olive skin, and a body that not only didn't quit, but was on permanent overtime. She could have had a sign around her neck that read: "One hundred percent woman."

In the course of the evening, Jack and I were looking lustily at Linda with our respective wives in attendance, not noticing our mutual attraction for this brown-haired bombshell.

Asa was feeling tired, now eight-and-a-half months pregnant, so I drove her home and put her to bed. Before she nodded off, I gently asked if she would mind my going back to the dinner party at Jack's.

"No, go ahead," said my ever-faithful wife. "Have a nice time."

I had arranged to meet up with Jack and Linda at the home she had shared with Tyrone Power on Copa De Ore Drive. I figured I'd find the two of them in her living room, sharing a drink, making small talk. When I arrived, I made my presence known.

"In here," I heard Jack yell.

I walked across the patio and into Linda's bedroom. The two were nude, wrapped in a warm embrace. Linda said, "Edd, take off your clothes and come join us." She didn't have to ask twice. To this day,

I think I set the *Guinness Book of World Records* for men's removal of clothing.

Linda had a king-sized bed and above the foot of it was a television. All the lights were off with the exception of the television. As I entered her, I opened my eyes and looked up at the television. Her deceased movie-star husband, Tyrone Power, appeared on the small screen. The title, now a household word: *Rawhide.*

The sex we had with her was incredible, with each movement performed with the grace and smoothness of a ballet dancer. It was very satisfying.

After having had sex for two hours, the three of us went to the bar for a drink. Linda had on a floor-length burgundy velvet dressing gown that accentuated her tiny little waist and made me hunger for her all the more. Even though this lady radiated an unmatched sexuality, I could still tell she was quite lonely. As she served us drinks, she said cryptically, "This is where Ty liked to entertain his guests and play bartender." Now that he was gone, Linda had taken his stead.

I felt guilty leaving my eight-and-a-half month pregnant wife for a ménage à trois. I rationalized my behavior by telling myself, *I guess I had a few too many drinks.*

A similar incident happened with actor Roger Moore when I visited him in London. This was way before Roger became James Bond. He was filming a television series called *The Persuaders* with Tony Curtis at Pinewood Studios. I called Roger to let him know I was in town.

"Come on by for lunch," my English friend insisted.

Roger was directing an episode, and he was very busy. But we managed to squeeze in lunch at the commissary.

We shared a lot of laughs together on the Warner Brothers lot when he was filming his television series, *The Alaskans.*

I visited with Tony Curtis for a bit. I've gotten to know Tony over the years. He's such an enthusiastic person about life; he has an abundant amount of energy. Tony is so underrated as an actor even though he's learned his craft so well and has been in some of the biggest movies of our time.

Tony starred in two pictures with Burt Lancaster, *Sweet Smell Of Success* and *Trapeze.* Tony was not always held in the highest regard concerning his acting, but he told me, "If you're up there with Burt Lancaster on the screen, people are going to realize you're not a bum." And he's absolutely right.

After his day's work of shooting, Roger decided that he didn't want to go straight home to his wife, Louisa. "Let's go out and celebrate," he suggested.

Roger and I drove in his Aston Martin to a quaint little restaurant where a young American actress happened to be nursing a drink. She was in her early twenties with a few films to her credit.

Roger and I took her back to my place. In no time, the actress had her clothes off, was under the covers, and was waiting for her two stars to take her to the galaxy.

Roger, ever the essence of the English gentleman, offered, "Go ahead old boy, you first."

Wanting to show that we Yanks could be just as polite as the Redcoats, I counteroffered, "No, Roger, you've been so hospitable all day, you first."

"I must insist, old boy."

"Roger . . . please, the young lady is waiting."

It was reminiscent of a many Marx Brothers routine, each insisting the other make the first move.

This was getting nowhere fast, and finally, our leading lady had enough of the pleasantries. She yelled out, "What the hell is wrong with you two? Are you gay?"

After our laughter subsided, the Yank and the Brit agreed to enter into a treaty, and we completed our threesome. The actress in question has yet to reach the stardom that we had predicted for her.

One thing about Roger Moore: He has a wicked sense of humor!

Another memorable time I had that involved London was on a plane trip I made in the late sixties. I was meeting John Harjes in Paris to collect a few antiques, but in order to get there, I had to fly to London first.

The plane was half full that day. As dinnertime approached, I noticed this very attractive woman sitting alone across the aisle. I asked her to join me, and we began to get acquainted. She told me her name was Janet. I then ordered a bottle of wine to add a touch of romance to the ambiance. As if this weren't enough, I pulled out a pair of my own set of candles and placed them on the tray as we were eating.

"I've never met anyone before who carries their own candles," Janet told me in all honesty. I must admit, I was always prepared for a romantic interlude.

As we finished dinner, the other passengers were getting ready to go to sleep. The lights on the plane were turned off, and the blankets and pillows were passed out.

This enchanting lady and I had the whole row to ourselves. I put up the armrests, and we lay down together, side by side. We began to cuddle and kiss, which eventually led to our lovemaking on the plane. It was the first time I had ever done anything like that.

I was on top of Janet when I received a tap on my shoulder. It was the captain of the plane.

"Yes?" I asked, wondering in that split second if the good pilot had heard I was aboard and was hoping to get an autograph at this most inconvenient time.

"Sir, some of the passengers are complaining about the noise," he said with a touch of disdain. I guess that meant he wasn't there for an autograph.

"What are you talking about?" I asked, playing coy.

"I think you know what I'm talking about, and I think you'd better stop," he said raising his voice and walking away.

My friend below me asked, "What was that all about?"

I hadn't had an orgasm yet, so I made up an excuse, "Oh, the captain wanted to know if I was comfortable," and went on making love. I did tell her, "Try not to make too much noise."

After we finished, I asked Janet, "So, what is it that you do for a living?"

"I work for this airline," she informed me.

"What?" I asked, almost astounded.

"I work for this airline flying back and forth from Los Angeles to London a couple of times a week to make sure that the service is right for the passengers."

I laughed out aloud, "You're kidding me, right?"

She assured me that it was her job to watch the flight attendants, making sure the passengers were well taken care of.

Right before we departed the plane, the stewardess asked me, "And how was the service, sir?"

"Very satisfying," I said, winking to my new friend.

* * * * *

Cheating, I discovered, not only had the potential of wreaking havoc on my marriage, but it could cost me my life.

I was in the lobby of the Beverly Hills Hotel cashing a check when I met Tita Barker, the wife of actor Lex Barker. Now Lex, you may recall, played Tarzan in a couple of movies and stood six feet four inches and 230 pounds. He was all muscle from head to toe and could pick me up by the neck and wring me out, were it his desire to do so.

Tita hailed from Spain and was a screaming siren. With big brown eyes, light-brown skin, she was a former beauty queen in her native

The early me. I celebrated my first birthday with a pony ride. That's me in the snow a month later. I was showing off my "yacht" when I was four.

A "formal" me (at right) with my mother and brother, Vinnie.

These were my first professional photos taken in Hollywood.

With George Brent, one of Hollywood's great movie idols. George was kind enough to explain a closeup to me.

Here with costar Dorothy Johnson in *Life Begins at 17*. Dorothy and I had a brief affair.

As I looked in *Darby's Rangers* with James Garner and French actress Etchika Chourea. Etchika married a Saudi Arabian prince after making this movie and was never heard from again(at least not in Hollywood).

And then The Big Break. Who would have thought a jive-talking, hair-combing parking-lot attendant would make me a star? Here I am taking a stroll in front of what became one of America's most famous addresses.

Taking a backseat to my friends and costars Efrem Zimbalist, Jr., (left) who played suave Stuart Bailey, former Ivy League professor, and Roger Smith, who was Jeff Spencer, onetime government undercover agent.

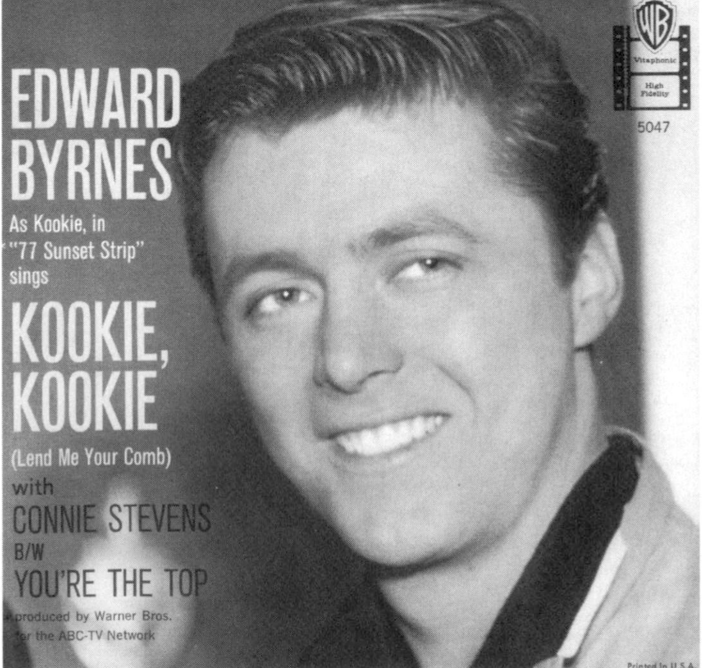

My first single record from Warner Brothers, which sold two million copies. What a miracle, considering what a singer I am.

At the height of my popularity, Warner Brothers was sending out fifteen thousand copies of this photo to fans—a week!

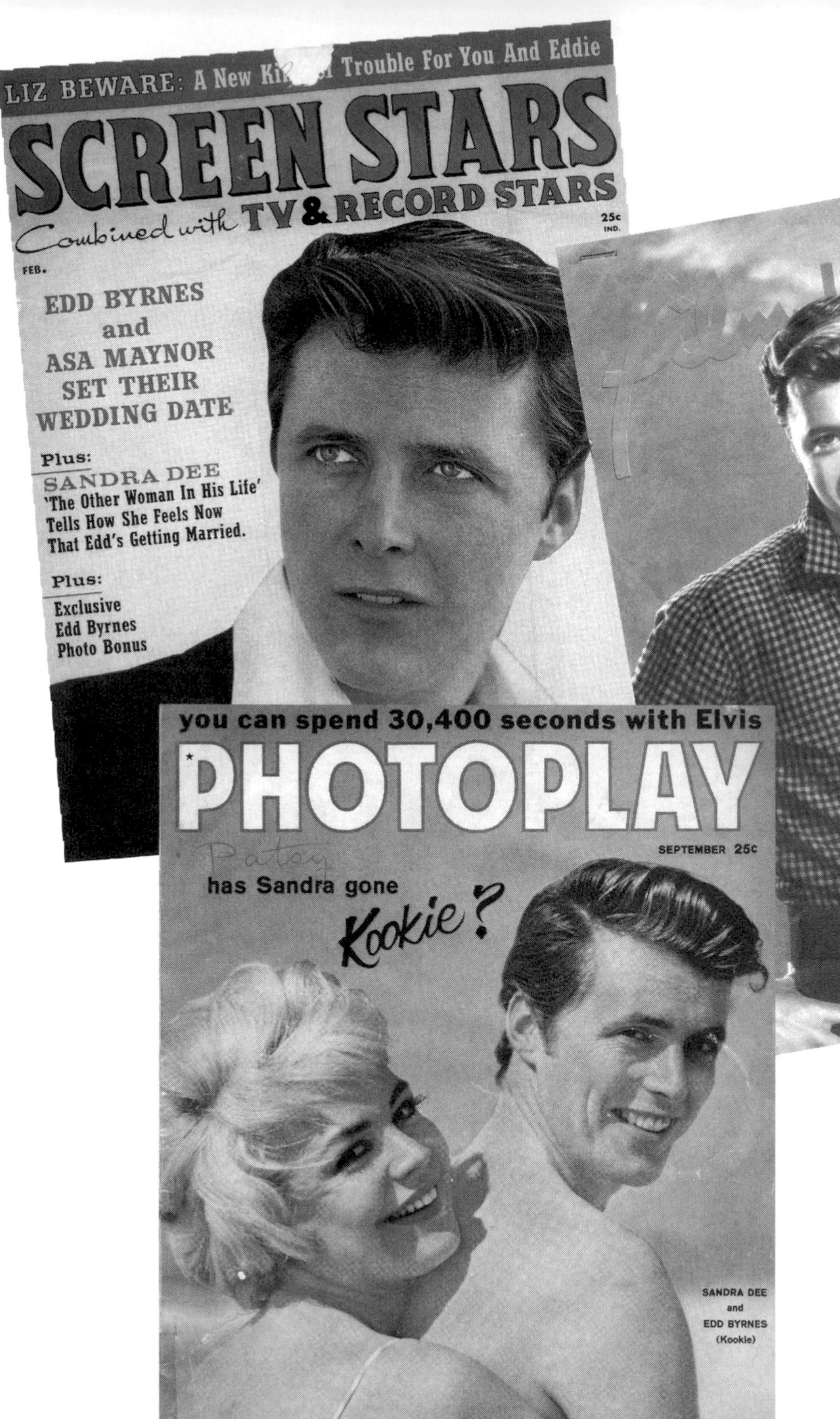
LIZ BEWARE: A New Ki[...] Trouble For You And Eddie
SCREEN STARS
Combined with TV & RECORD STARS
25c
IND.
FEB.
EDD BYRNES
and
ASA MAYNOR
SET THEIR
WEDDING DATE
Plus:
SANDRA DEE
'The Other Woman In His Life'
Tells How She Feels Now
That Edd's Getting Married.
Plus:
Exclusive
Edd Byrnes
Photo Bonus
you can spend 30,400 seconds with Elvis
PHOTOPLAY
SEPTEMBER 25c
has Sandra gone
Kookie?
SANDRA DEE
and
EDD BYRNES
(Kookie)

My face began gracing the covers of national and international magazines.

Riding the crest of my popularity in the early sixties, here I'm having dinner with Frank Sinatra and Sandra Dee at Puccini's, his restaurant in Beverly Hills. Frank asked me to costar with him, Sammy Davis, Jr., Peter Lawford, and Dean Martin in *Ocean's 11.*

At a dinner party with Mr. and Mrs. Danny Thomas, given for Danny's favorite charity, St. Jude (circa 1962).

If you're riding high, you might as well ride in style. Here I'm heading into my driveway in my new 1962, racing-green Jaguar. I always did fancy English cars and English women.

Till death do us part or so we thought.
Asa and me getting married, March 1962,
in Beverly Hills.

My favorite picture of Asa, taken around 1968.

In a scene from *The Secret Invasion* with Mickey Rooney. Mickey was a true wild man, a real genius, and great fun to be around. We shared many bottles of wine.

Me in *The Alfred Hitchcock Hour* (circa 1964). The episode, called "The Final Escape," is one that many fans bring up.

In *Yellowstone Kelly* (1960). At this time, I had a hit film, TV series, and million-selling record. My career was red hot!

Stewart Granger and I clashed when he tried to cut my dialogue from this scene in *The Secret Invasion* (1964).

That's me, Logan, and Asa on the left and Natalie Wood with her then-husband, Richard Gregson, on the right, in 1969. Natalie was Logan's godmother and a close, dear friend.

With my son, Logan, on location in Del Coronado, California, while I was filming *Wicked, Wicked* (1968) for MGM.

Tennis with Kirk Douglas at the Riviera Hotel in Las Vegas. That's a vodka and orange juice I'm nursing (1976).

George Hamilton turning his script over to me in Neil Simon's *The Star Spangled Girl* at the Drury Lane Theater in Chicago (1971).

Visiting R. J. Wagner on the set of his TV series, *It Takes a Thief.* R. J. can charm the birds right out of the trees.

With baseball great Mickey Mantle and TV host Merv Griffin, in the early seventies. After the show, Mickey and I enjoyed a double date with two gorgeous airline stewardesses.

Rehearsal with Stockard Channing (left) and Dinah Manoff in *Grease*. This movie was the highest-grossing musical of all time.

As Vince Fontaine, hip-hopping, be-bopping, fast-talking host of *National Bandstand.* And awaaaay we go!

With young, delicious, eighteen-year-old Heather Locklear on the set of *Twirl*, an ABC Movie of the Week (1980).

Liza Minnelli and me at her opening night at the Riviera Hotel in Las Vegas. Drinking Diet Coke and enjoying our sobriety (1992).

Logan and me in 1995. It's an honor and a privilege to be his father.

land. She was so stunning, she could have stopped rush-hour traffic in New York City.

We began a casual conversation at the front desk of the hotel. I happened to mention that I was headed for Hawaii the next day to promote my new movie, *Wicked, Wicked* for MGM.

Tita squealed with delight, "I'm going to Hawaii tomorrow, too!"

"You're kidding? I'd love to see you while I'm there. Could I take you to lunch?"

"I'd love it!"

I mentioned to Tita that I was staying at the Outrigger Hotel and suggested she call me when she got into town. I didn't think she would, but she did.

Tita arrived in Hawaii with a friend named Mercedes, and they were staying in a condominium together. Mercedes was a good friend of Tita's, but secretly had the hots for her husband, Lex.

During the week, I did some interviews with the local papers and plugged *Wicked, Wicked.* It was the least I could do for MGM since they were paying for my suite and all of my expenses. Mr. Mayer was probably turning over in his grave.

Tita came to my hotel that first night, and we had a romantic candlelight dinner with a bright full moon looking down on us. After I paid the bill, we went for a walk on the beach. It was a balmy night, and we hugged and kissed passionately. Our temperatures started to rise. She was a very sensual woman, and she melted into my arms.

We decided rather than make love on the sand, we would take off all our clothes, swim out to one of the empty boats on the water, and fulfill each other's desires there. Having gotten undressed, we walked into the water up to our waists, looked at each other, and said, "This is toooo cold!" We went back to the beach, got dressed, and headed directly to my penthouse suite with its king-sized bed.

Tita was crazy, wild, and absolutely adored me. She was also a bit sexually advanced for her time. We began to make love when my former beauty queen requested an odd favor of me.

"Edd, would you please spank me?"

"Come again?" I asked, nearly choking.

"Hit me, Edd. I want you to hit me. Spank me, Edd."

This was far out, but I didn't want to hit this gorgeous creature. "Tita, I don't want to hurt you. Why on earth would you want me to hit you?"

"I've been a bad girl."

I knew there must have been a reasonable explanation.

So I complied with her wishes and began spanking her, but this wasn't enough for my wild lover.

"Harder, Edd, harder!" This woman could take a hit. I'd put up even money on her if she had to go up against Ali, Frazier, or Tyson.

After our rough session of lovemaking, I looked at her buttocks and legs and spotted innumerable bruises.

"My God! Tita, look at your legs. What's Lex going to say?"

"Don't worry about Lex, I can take care of him," the little sexpot proclaimed.

Meanwhile, Tita's *good* friend, Mercedes, had the perfect opportunity to make her move on Lex. She ratted us out like a paid informant on *America's Most Wanted.*

"Lex, Tita's been sleeping with Edd Byrnes the whole week," Mercedes told the muscleman in Los Angeles over the phone.

Tita and I had arranged to fly back together, and our affair continued in Los Angeles. Asa wasn't around, so Tita spent the night with me, and I received a phone call at about 6:00 A.M.

"Hello?" I answered groggily.

"Edd!" said a powerful voice on the other end of the phone.

"Yeah?"

"This is Lex Barker."

HELLO AND GOOD MORNING! It was the wake-up call of my life.

Tarzan the Ape Man continued this most auspicious phone call, "Edd, I know you've been fucking my wife. I know where you live. I've got a gun. It's loaded. I'M COMING OVER TO GET YOU NOW."

Click!

No need for the morning English breakfast tea to wake me up. This was quite enough, thank you. I jumped out of bed and told Tita to grab her things and get dressed fast.

"What's wrong, darling?"

"Lex has a gun and is on his way over to pay us a visit. I don't think it's a social call."

We got in my black Studebaker Hawk and tore out of the driveway like it was the Batmobile exit. I headed straight toward Malibu. I don't know why Malibu, it just seemed logical at the time. While I was on the road, I came up with a plan. I'd drive to Stuart Whitman's home, who happened to live in Malibu with his wife, Caroline.

Let me say at this point that Tita was about to leave Lex, but that didn't make what I was doing morally proper or correct. I just want to point out that I wasn't breaking up a marriage or anything like that; yet it remained that this man was out to snap me in half like a number two pencil.

I called Stu from a pay telephone on Pacific Coast Highway.

"Stu? Edd Byrnes here. I've got a small problem. I'm with Lex Barker's wife, Tita, and we've been sleeping together in Hawaii for the past week. Lex is a little upset."

"I'd say you have a big problem, pardner," Stu replied. "Eddie, maybe you'd better come over."

Stu, knowing Lex, offered to help me out. We arrived at the Whitman's and came clean about our relationship. Caroline came up with the idea that we would say that we both happened to fly back together on the same flight from Hawaii. On the plane, I offered to drive Tita to the Whitman's home where she spent the night.

Tita then called Lex from Stuart's place. "Hello, darling Lex? It's Tita. Would you please come and pick me up at Stuart and Caroline Whitman's in Malibu?"

I could hear Lex's voice on the other end, something about, "Edd Byrnes . . . dead man . . . ten o'clock news . . . "

Tita, wielding the power of a persuasive pussycat, calmed down Mr. Ape Man. "Lex, where do you get such ideas? No, sweetie, I'm over at Stuart and Caroline's in Malibu. Edd just happened to be on the plane and was sweet enough to drive me over to Stu's. Don't be so jealous, just come and get me, my darling."

There was still one little thing to get past Lex, Tita's profound bruises. Ah, but Ms. Barker was a sneaky little devil. The next day when she came over to my place, I asked her how she handled Lex. She told me that when she got home, she began to kiss Lex and proceeded to get him excited. Tita was wearing a skirt that day and requested to be spanked, only this time, through her skirt. Lex obliged and spanked his naughty little girl good and hard. When Tita lifted her skirt, she acted shocked and scolded her beefy husband, "You brute! Look at these bruises! How could you have done this to me?"

What an actress!

Now and again, I would run into Lex at the Los Angeles Tennis Club. He wasn't a tennis player, but he loved backgammon. He didn't lay a hand on me, but he always looked at me with a jaundiced eye.

Lex and Tita were still married when walking down Fifth Avenue in New York to a luncheon; he died of a heart attack. I don't know if it was from a bad ticker or his bad wife, but Tita Barker could have given any man a heart attack. She later married a baron from Spain who's so wealthy that he lent out part of his collection to the Prado

Museum in Madrid. So far, his heart seems to be holding up pretty well. I hope she's been a good little girl all of these years and hasn't needed a spanking, but I do miss her.

I soon discovered that the night life on the Sunset Strip was also a playground for sex and drugs. Coffeehouses and nightclubs dominated the Strip in the sixties. The Chez Paulette was a place we occasionally filmed in the series, and it was an actors' hangout as well. Dennis Hopper, Lenny Bruce, Sally Kellerman, and Sal Mineo could be found there all the time.

The Whiskey A Go-Go, the Daisy, and the Rainbow were very popular nightclubs at the time. The Rainbow was a place where you could always score marijuana, cocaine, or young girls.

It was a young woman, a hippie actually, I picked up in one of these clubs who introduced me to amyl nitrate. In the middle of having intercourse, she asked me to inform her when I reached the point of orgasm. As I did, I heard a "pop" and I was told to inhale this strange drug.

"Here, take a sniff," she ordered.

She shoved the vial under my nose and I breathed in deeply. I began to see stars. I thought the top of my head was going to come off. Amyl nitrate is used to revive heart-attack patients and can kill you if you inhale too much of the stuff.

Sex parties also surfaced in the Hollywood hills of the rich and famous. Every Saturday night, a particular mansion would be rented out, and normally you had to bring a date. Because I was widely known, I was exempt from that rule and enjoyed the fruits of these parties.

The top floor was like cocktail hour at a bar with beautiful women all over the place. There'd be a buffet table with food, people on sofas talking, a fireplace that warmed the house, and a bar that served any drink and rivaled a legitimate pub.

The bottom floor was more or less a den of iniquity. Moans and groans filled the air as couples had sex with strangers, each other's wives, men with women, women with women, two men and one woman, two women with one man, any combination one could imagine went on in the place.

My thing was having one woman at a time, although I wouldn't turn down two if offered the opportunity. It wasn't unusual for someone to make love to three different women before the light of day introduced itself.

One night, the music was too loud in the mansion, and the cops had to come inside the place. I thought we were all going to get busted, and those weren't headlines I wanted to make. I was heading towards the back door when I heard the cops laughing it up. They told us that it wasn't illegal to host such a party, but just to turn down the music. This was the kind of call the cops needed to "lift" their spirits on an otherwise boring night in the wealthiest zip code in the country.

Of course, all of this was before AIDS had entered into the picture, but that was a typical Saturday night in Beverly Hills.

As crazy as this sounds, I loved Asa very much, but I also loved the company of other women and partying till dawn. It still happens today with a lot of major stars. Actors on the whole are an insecure lot. Once thrown into the spotlight, they are like kids in a candy store. Suddenly, the spoils of fame are handed to them, like Eve offering Adam the apple in the Garden of Eden. You'd be surprised at the stars who parade around on television, proclaiming they're family men, who were no different than me. Very surprised. It takes quite a man to resist such temptation, and I was not such a man.

I knew that if somehow our marriage was going to work, I'd have to be a little faithful to Asa, but that's like being a "little pregnant."

Speaking of being pregnant, Asa gave birth to our only son, Logan, on September 13, 1965.

Asa, Natalie, and I were all in Natalie's sauna the night before Asa gave birth. It was 5:00 A.M. when I put Asa in the Jaguar to take her to the hospital, only I was so nervous I got lost on the way.

After many U-turns and running red lights, we finally made it to the emergency entrance of the hospital. Asa was put in a wheelchair and taken to be prepped for delivery. I was left alone in the waiting room to wait.

The sun was coming up, and I was looking out of the window, watching the city wake up. I saw some pigeons flying below and was mesmerized by the stillness of the morning. I felt different somehow. The doctor came in and said, "Congratulations, Mr. Byrnes, you have a son." He then asked if I would like to see him.

They had our baby wrapped in a blanket in the delivery room and from the moment I laid eyes on him, I loved him and that love has continued to grow every day.

Our son didn't have a name for a few days. We had chosen a name for a girl, Bentley Byrnes, but we didn't have one for a boy. Asa was still in recovery, calling me on the phone, asking, "Have you thought of a name yet?"

"No. For some reason, I'm having a block."

"Well, I just saw a nurse, and as she handed me the baby, I noticed the badge on her uniform. It read 'Mrs. Logan.' What do you think of the name Logan for the baby?"

"That's it! That's it! Logan."

We were living in Benedict Canyon, so we added Benedict as his middle name. It was official: Logan Benedict Byrnes. I liked the idea of giving him his own name. I didn't want him to become Edd Byrnes, Jr. I think it's a horrible thing to make your son a Junior, especially if the father is famous. I thought Logan was a very strong name and with a name like that, he couldn't help but be a success, which he is today.

Despite my philandering ways, I was thrilled to be a parent. I vowed to be there for my son, unlike my father before me.

CHAPTER ELEVEN

My Four Drinking Buddies

JOHN HARJES AND I stayed in touch throughout the years after I left New York. There was nothing sexual between us any longer, and if anything, this man had become the closest thing I had to a father.

I bought my second home after Logan was born. John offered to furnish the house with antiques for me. His French aunt had passed on, leaving everything in her will to John. John invited me to France to take whatever I wanted out of her castle. "OK Eddie, go get what you want," and he was very encouraging. I picked out a few things, some rugs, some paintings, a couple of cases of wine, and a very expensive antique desk that I still have to this day. I spent several thousand dollars shipping the antiques back to the States, but that's how much John liked giving things away. He relished bringing joy to people.

Asa and I even went on a vacation with John. He invited us to be his guests in Guadeloupe, a French island in the Caribbean. We flew first class, and by this time, John was carrying a flask of vodka with him everywhere he went.

After leaving Miami, we arrived in Guadeloupe. Asa and I were in the room next to John's in the hotel. My wife and I noticed a lot of frogs on this island. When John was out and about, we rounded up all the frogs we could find and put them in John's bed underneath his sheets.

The next morning at breakfast, John asked, "Do you have any frogs in your room?"

It was all Asa and I could do to keep our food down, but we managed to fake a sincere, "No. Not at all. Why do you ask?"

"This damn island must be infested with frogs because I found them in my bed and all over the room."

He didn't even suspect that we could be the culprits behind such a devious act, so Asa and I kept up the ritual every night until we left. At the end of our stay, John went up to the concierge and complained about the frogs. I couldn't stifle my laughter any longer, and I confessed to him that we were the evil frognappers. Much to my surprise, he didn't laugh at our sophomoric prank. It seemed the alcohol made him lose his sense of humor.

As an adult, I had not seen firsthand how the devastating effects of alcohol can physically deteriorate a human being, that is, until I saw John for the last time.

Asa, Logan, and I were visiting the East Coast on vacation, and I decided to stop by and visit John at his farm in New Jersey. He had all types of animals on his land, including zebras, llamas, sheep, and an aviary full of exotic birds. I thought it would be a fun experience for Logan to pet these friendly creatures.

I had been to the farm many times before, and almost every one of John's houseguests and neighbors, who were all very wealthy, were heavy drinkers. The local doctor, Don, and John's wife, Jean, were big boozers. John was the bartender. He would pour these potent drinks of half orange juice and half vodka. They were so strong that his guests, who usually wouldn't refuse a drink, disposed of them into the plants when John wasn't looking. Even his plants were getting sauced every night. His drinking had escalated to the point where he was the King of the Mountain and put the other heavy drinkers to shame.

When John greeted us at the door, I knew I was shaking hands with a dead man.

His physical deterioration shook me so badly, I took him aside and cautioned, "John, you've got to stop drinking!" He was up to a quart of vodka a day and was beckoning death with both hands outstretched and both feet already in the grave.

In desperation, John replied, "Eddie, it's my only pleasure in life."

In addition to his drinking problem, John suffered from diabetes and high blood pressure, which in combination with vodka straight up is simply lethal.

I was uneducated in the ways of alcoholism and was unfamiliar with 12-step programs. Therefore, I could not offer him any solutions. I could only plead my case in desperation. "Listen to me, John. You've got this beautiful farm, your friends, your animals, you don't ever have to worry financially, you've got everything!!!"

"Yes, I do, but none of those things give me any pleasure." He held up his glass of poison, looked at me with a cold stare, and said, "This does."

John Harjes died ten days later at the age of fifty-six. John was living with a bodybuilder named Jonathan whom he picked up at the Plaza Hotel, showered with gifts, and made his new boyfriend. It was Jonathan who wrote to me about John's death.

I took the news extremely hard and oh, how I cried. It was as if my father had died. I shed genuine tears when John Harjes died, whereas I didn't when my real father passed on.

* * * * *

Around the early sixties, I became friendly with actors David Janssen, Laurence Harvey, William Holden, and businessman Ralph Stolkin.

Nearly every weekend in the winter, all four of us would retreat to Palm Springs with our wives and meet at Ralph's house on Rimrock Drive. It was a luxurious home with tall wraparound windows, giving a 180-degree view of Palm Springs. It was simply magnificent.

Ralph Stolkin was the man who supposedly invented the ballpoint pen, but there was talk he had ties with the Mafia back in Chicago. He had surveillance cameras everywhere and very tight security, including bodyguards. It definitely made me wonder if the rumors were true.

Mr. Stolkin also employed a full-time chef who was paid one thousand dollars a week to cook his meals. Not a bad paycheck for the early sixties, but Ralph's eating habits were peculiar. He would only eat tuna-fish salads. I once commented, "Geez, Ralph, you pay this guy a grand a week and all you do is eat tuna-fish salads. I can make that!" (The money almost matched my contract at Warner Brothers in its last year!) Ralph's guests were the only ones who enjoyed exotic gourmet meals at his home.

I bought most of my wine from Laurence Harvey. He had his own winery in the Napa Valley, and naturally, a friendship evolved. Larry owned two homes in Palm Springs and let Asa and I stay in one of them on weekends.

It was through Ralph Stolkin that I met William Holden. Bill lived down the street, and he, Larry, David Janssen, and I would meet at Ralph's for drinks and dinner parties. My four drinking buddies, what a sight to behold!

It was there that Larry introduced me to the Bullshot. The drink consisted of vodka, beef bouillon, lemon juice, and Tabasco sauce. From the first sip, I was hooked. Incidentally, that was Larry's Sunday morning drink to get him out of bed.

Larry was a funny guy, but he had this weird quirk where he would try to sell you anything. If he hadn't been an actor, you would have sworn he was a used-car salesman. All he needed was a pair of white patent-leather shoes, and you wouldn't have known the difference.

Once while I was at his home, I was in need of a television set. I was in his maid's room, and I spotted a nice big TV. I was teasing Larry when I told him I didn't have a television set at all, adding, "Why don't you sell me your maid's television set?" By golly, wouldn't you know it? He sold it to me. Later, as I was leaving, the maid saw me carrying her television and had the most bewildered look on her face as I headed out the door. Larry always had a price. Anything in his house was for sale.

Mr. Harvey was also the most hedonistic man I had ever met. I once had a ménage à trois with Larry in London. He was performing in *Camelot* (he was constantly singing along to the Richard Burton album in his home) when I went to visit him backstage at the West End in London. We had dinner at his favorite restaurant in Soho. As we were walking back to his apartment on Park Lane, we picked up a girl who recognized us.

The three of us were drinking and dancing, the knickers came off, and eventually we found ourselves naked and enjoying ourselves immensely. A little later on in the evening, the door opened. It was Larry's fiancée, model Pauline Stone. She walked in on us in bed, not in the act mind you, but the smell of sex was definitely lingering in the air. Somehow Larry managed to smooth things over by telling her that this girl was with me and that he didn't want to be a rude host. He said he wanted his guests to be comfortable and if they had their clothes off, well, he should have his clothes off as well. To my amazement (and to Larry's relief), she bought it hook, line, and sinker. I told you he was an excellent salesman.

They say that the opposite of love is not hate, but indifference, and that's how Larry felt about most women. He later married Harry Cohn's wife, Joan. Joan was a wealthy Beverly Hills socialite who tried in vain to keep their marriage together. She was always crying to me, "I don't know what to do about Larry. I can never have dinner alone with him. Since we've been married, I haven't had one night alone with him." I felt for Joan because Larry always wanted to be with people. He'd have dinner with eight to twenty people every night, and would go out on the prowl with his friends, drinking, carousing, partying, or chasing other women.

As much as Larry was a womanizer, I strongly suspected he was bisexual. Though he never put the make on me, Larry was always up for anything that felt good.

I have a gut feeling that Larry may have been having an affair with James Wolf, his sponsor/benefactor/film producer throughout the years. Jimmy was responsible for casting him in meaty acting roles, including *Room at the Top,* Larry's breakthrough role.

Though he was always a fun guy to be around, I sensed Larry was a tortured soul, as are most alcoholics. I don't think he was ever truly happy. He pretended to enjoy life when he was really running from it. He was always racing from one place to another.

David and Ellie Janssen lived down the street from us in Coldwater Canyon when David was working on the series, *The Fugitive.* Asa and Ellie became very close, and the four of us spent a lot of time together in Palm Springs.

David Janssen (David Meyer was his real name) was the only actor I ever knew who could sit and drink wine all day, then perform a five-page scene of dialogue and remember it cold. He wouldn't get that drunk, but he stayed nice and slightly "buzzed" all day. He could drink and work without a hitch, something that I could never do.

Whenever I'd visit David on a set, I could always count on opening his dressing-room refrigerator and finding a chilled bottle of vodka or white wine. Really, he kept every kind of booze a man could ask for. Hollywood had never seen a better-stocked dressing-room bar.

As much as he drank, David was a kind man who was always a considerate host, and he possessed a wonderful sense of humor.

William Holden was a man that I admired greatly, not only because of his incredible body of work, but because it was a sincere pleasure to be around him. When I think of Bill Holden, I think of the play *The Pleasure of His Company.* While I was in Munich, he invited me to the set of *13 Hours of Munich,* a movie of the week about the Israeli commandos during the 1972 Olympics.

I spent the afternoon with him. He was always joking about and remaining so courteous to everyone around him. He teased the director, "I know you originally wanted Bob Mitchum for this role, but he asked too much money, so you settled on me." He had a great self-deprecating kind of humor.

I remember an amusing anecdote he once told me about the making of *The Wild Bunch,* one of my favorite movies of all time. Bill told me he used to try to find ways to steal a scene from Ernest Borgnine, but he never could. If you watch the film closely, you'll see what he means.

When I met him in Germany, Bill had been sober for three years and looked terrific. He was in fantastic shape for a man in his late fifties. As he was getting fitted for his wardrobe, I jokingly told him that he still had the same body he did when he played Hal Carter in *Picnic.* He looked fit and tan and seemed to be very content with himself.

On that same trip, I was staying in the same hotel, the Bayerischer Hof, as Muhammad Ali. He was fighting Richard Dunn on May 24, 1976, for the heavyweight championship of the world. One of Ali's entourage asked me, "Would you like to meet the Champ?"

"Hell, yeah!" I said excitedly. I am a huge fan of boxing and, in meeting Ali, there could be no greater thrill for me.

I was escorted to his suite. Ali was gorging himself with food. He ate enough for five people. His meal included two dinner salads, two steaks, two desserts, five helpings of vegetables and after his meal, he swallowed around fifty vitamin pills.

Candice Bergen was there covering Ali on an assignment for *Life* magazine. Ali was so funny, full of wit, and charming beyond what one might expect of a boxer. Larger than life itself. At the dinner table, he said to Candice in that sweet tone of his, "Whoooo Candice, we'd make a beautiful baby together. C'mon, sugar, let's get into bed together. What a beautiful baby we'd have! Ooooh, you be so white, and I'm so black. Can you imagine how pretty our child would be?" The Champ had us in hysterics.

I've seen Ali since, and he's obviously changed. Still as sweet as ever, but just not the once-vibrant man he used to be. The years in the ring have obviously taken their toll on the greatest boxer in history.

As for my four drinking buddies, life took a toll on them as well. They all died of alcohol-related causes.

In the end, Ralph Stolkin never got out of his pajamas and bathrobe. He stayed inside all day and drank until he passed out. His live-in girlfriend didn't call an ambulance when he actually died because she thought he had once again just passed out. To her, it was business as usual. She left him lying there for a few hours. An autopsy later showed that he choked on his own vomit.

Laurence Harvey, like John Harjes, had everything a man could ever want in the way of wealth, but died from liver cancer at forty-six. I imagine that it was brought on by his days of excessive drinking.

David Janssen died of a heart attack at 5:00 A.M. in his sleep. I can personally attest to the fact it was from a combination of overworking himself, lack of exercise, not enough rest, and of course, the heavy drinking. David never took the time to stop and smell the roses. He was working all the time as if he felt he was never going to work again. When he wasn't filming his series, *Harry-O*, he'd be filming a movie of the week. Poor David was forty-nine years old when his heart gave out.

Asa and I attended David's memorial service along with several hundred of his friends who showed up to pay their respects. Abbey Greshler, David's longtime agent, greeted friends and showed them to their pews. I couldn't help but think, *There's good ol' Abbey, still working for David even after he's gone.*

After the service, one of David's good friends, Stan Herman, threw a party in David's honor. David would have loved it. The booze was flowing, and the food and people were outstanding. It was a happy and jovial time with everyone reminiscing about David. It was something of an Irish wake.

My turn came, and I told of how David always wore top-of-the-line tennis apparel, but mysteriously, when he played, he never broke a sweat. Finally my curiosity got the best of me, and I had asked him, "David, you play tennis all of the time, but I never see you sweat. What's the deal?"

David had smiled and boldly stated, "Edd, movie stars don't sweat." The entire house burst out laughing.

After a while, I migrated downstairs to a guest bedroom where I found Jack Lemmon and Michelle Phillips reminiscing about our dearly departed. After a few minutes, Michelle broke out a joint, and the three of us indulged. Of course, this was after much wine. We were feeling quite chummy, and Jack and I were becoming very affectionate with Michelle, but nothing ever came of it. I went upstairs and left the two to themselves. I'm sure David would have approved of our behavior that day—he always loved to have a good time when he wasn't working.

As for Bill Holden, he fell off the wagon and began to drink again. After a few days of drinking in his Santa Monica Ocean Avenue apartment, Bill slipped and fell, cutting his head open on an end table next to his bed. He bled to death. The path of alcohol led him to an early grave.

Of that group of five drinkers, I am the only one still alive.

* * * * *

The toll the alcohol was taking on my personal life was mounting. The substance was sapping my once-ravenous sex drive, and I was beginning to neglect Asa. Not only sexually, but emotionally as well.

Additional damage had been done by Asa's psychiatrist. He was feeding her the line that she was not having a proper orgasm with me. She was having an outer orgasm, but not an inner orgasm. Huh? Is there *really* a difference? Isn't an orgasm an orgasm?

Many nights, I would pass out on the sofa and sleep there instead of lying next to my wife and making love to her. Asa suggested we have a three-month trial separation, and I was shocked.

In my anger, I called my psychiatrist, Ernie White. "Ernie, why didn't you tell me my marriage was breaking up?" I scolded him like a child. I expected him to say, "Edd, you'd better start paying closer attention to your wife." If he did tell me, I didn't hear it.

Asa told me years later the main problem in our marriage was that I didn't listen. I was so focused on myself and my career that I seldom paid much attention to her. I just assumed that she would be grateful for our lifestyle and that it would make up for whatever I couldn't give to her emotionally. The first seven years of our marriage had been exciting and fun. I figured it would go on forever.

She complained that a dog we had, a Saint Bernard, received more of my affection than she did. She was probably right.

"Either the dog goes or I go," was her ultimatum. I wanted our marriage to work, so I gave my beloved dog to composer Quincy Jones, who lived up the street from us. That way, I could still visit the dog when I wanted.

Despite the cheating and running around, I dearly loved Asa. I also enjoyed my home life and my family. We'd always have friends over to drink, barbecue, eat, and swim. My family gave me the stability that I had always wanted as a child. I was deeply in love with her, but the alcoholic fog that surrounded me masked her words, "Edd, you've got to change. I'm really unhappy with our situation." The message went in one ear and out the other, and I went about with my "business as usual" attitude.

Asa gave me three months to shape up or ship out. Guess what I did? I shipped out. I felt that Logan needed his mother and a home, so I left our beautiful home a dejected man.

Quincy Jones was good enough to put me up in his guesthouse for a few weeks while Asa and I tried to work things out. It was a strange situation, because Quincy was married to actress Peggy Lipton, with whom I had an affair only a few years earlier.

There was tremendous pain in leaving my house, Asa, and especially, having to leave Logan. I felt so guilty about my son; I too often thought, *Logan's going to grow up without a father, just like I did.*

My whole world caved in. To deaden the pain I was feeling, marked by a constant churning in the pit of my stomach, alcohol was the only way out for me. I knew that it was the only thing that would numb the pain. In Quincy's guesthouse, I was drinking white wine all day, followed by a couple of sleeping pills to allow me to sleep. And come morning, it was vodka or rum to get me going.

I thought that by staying at Quincy's, Asa would miss me and thus see how we belonged together. If anything, it made our situation worse.

I found out the hard way that when Asa cuts someone off, it's over. The umbilical cord is severed and you're left to float off into space all alone. When Asa makes up her mind, man or woman, friend or foe, and cuts someone off, that's it. The end, period, and three exclamation points.

In a way, I admire her for that. I would have been content to hang on, to stay in a miserable situation, even if it's painful, because at least it's familiar. But not her, brother. Personally, I hate changes.

Sensing I wasn't progressing the way she would have liked, Asa delivered a verbal blow that I didn't recover from for a full decade.

"You've had plenty of time to get yourself together, but I see you've only gotten worse. You haven't been listening for the last three months, so I want you to listen very closely to this, I WANT A DIVORCE!"

For once, my hearing was sufficiently clear.

CHAPTER TWELVE

London Calling

AS IF I HADN'T infuriated my dear wife enough, I went out and hired an attorney to represent me, one James Cantalin, who was the same attorney that Asa wanted to represent her.

Jim Cantalin was highly regarded around town as a divorce lawyer, and acting immediately, I put him on retainer.

A few days later, Asa called Jim on the telephone.

"Jim, I would like you to represent me in divorce proceedings against my husband, Edd Byrnes," she informed him.

She was in for a real shocker. "Asa, I can't represent you."

"Well, why not?"

"I'm already representing Edd."

God, couldn't I do anything right? I couldn't even hire a divorce lawyer without ticking off my wife.

It took Asa about a year to actually serve me with the divorce papers. If she had had it her way, it would have happened much sooner than that.

After six weeks of staying in Quincy Jones's guesthouse, I decided to move into an apartment in the Hollywood Hills. That was one of many apartments I lived in that year in my attempt to avoid the inevitable divorce papers that Asa wanted to have served. I always stayed one step ahead of her and that didn't win me any brownie points, either. I didn't want a divorce. I would have never left our house if I'd have had it my way. My family was always very important to me. I knew I was a sick man who needed help. I was always hoping for a reconciliation, but Asa must have had a crystal ball, because I didn't get any better in the ensuing years. In fact, Asa had met somebody already, Michael Tennenbaum, a successful stockbroker in Century City.

I had seen Michael around our house a few times, and my first thought was to pick up a baseball bat and break his legs. I was extremely jealous of him. I later came to my senses and realized that Michael had nothing to do with breaking up my marriage. Eventually, Michael became a good friend and tennis partner. A few years later, Asa cut him off as well. She was actually upset that we had become friends. When Asa gave him the ax treatment, Michael came to me for advice and consolation. A strange world, indeed.

In Italy, the family is what society values. In America, it seems like it's the least important. Statistics now show that one out of every two marriages in the United States will end in divorce. My family meant such a great deal to me because I was raised in a dysfunctional home. I never had a real family, and that's what I wanted more than anything in the whole world. All I ever wanted was to love somebody and have them love me back. That's probably why I became an actor. If I'm in the movies, people will love and remember me, and I'll never die.

I had successfully avoided being served divorce papers for one full year when Rod Serling offered me a part in his only play, *Storm in Summer*. The part was for a lot less money than I usually got, but it was a Rod Serling play. At the very least, I was working, with something to keep my mind occupied.

The play opened in San Diego, and one of my costars was Sam Jaffe. Sam was one fine actor in his heyday and had played Dr. David Zorba on *Ben Casey*. Mr. Jaffe was verging on elderly, or had nudged past it, by the time I worked with him. Sam, God bless him, never could remember the script. Up until opening night, he kept flubbing his lines. When it's just you and another actor up there on stage, you know when your counterpart doesn't know his lines. That's what we call in this business "panic time." I knew the poor guy's lines better than he did.

It got so bad that his wife was on the side of the stage, in the wings, cuing Sam, trying to whisper his lines to him. Did I forget to mention that Sam was also hard of hearing? Definitely "panic time."

We rehearsed hard for five weeks, and still, Sam wasn't getting it. This made for one anxious Edd on opening night. I just knew that I was going to have to improvise and cover for him. Just when I thought it couldn't get any worse, as I was putting on my makeup for opening night, three burly county marshals barged into my dressing room.

"Mr. Byrnes?"

Gulp . . . "Yes?"

"On behalf of Ms. Asa Maynor, we hereby serve you with these divorce proceedings."

BAM! Shot down on the spot, and not with some puny 12-gauge, but a 155 howitzer!

Talk about a downer, of all of the times to serve a husband, why on opening night? That was the absolute worst time to serve me divorce papers. I guess I asked for it. I avoided Asa as much as I could, so you might say that I had it coming to me.

Either Asa or one of her friends read in the newspaper that I was going to appear in the play, and it would be the only possible time to serve me. They call that, folks, *Divorce: Hollywood Style.*

My nightmare still wasn't over. After the play (yes, Sam did flub a few lines, but that seemed so minute after what had just transpired),

Rod Serling hosted an opening-night party. I had a new girlfriend on my arm, Marti, and we were drinking wine until it ran out. I volunteered to chase down a few more bottles at the liquor store, and Marti and I went in my car.

In those days, I wasn't a bar drinker, I was a car drinker. To drink and drive was no big deal for me. So I opened a bottle of wine on the way back to the party. All of a sudden, these red flashing lights appeared out of nowhere, and the police signaled for me to pull over.

Marti was wearing a dress that night, and I asked her to hide the open bottle between her legs.

The police officer came up to my window and asked if I had had anything to drink, to which I casually replied, "Yeah, a little glass of wine." The real truth was, a lot of little glasses of wine. He then asked Marti to step out of the car. When she did, the bottle crashed to the ground and shattered in little pieces.

Luckily, I passed the sobriety test, but the officer issued me a citation for having an open container of alcohol in the car. I later had an attorney take care of the situation and never had to appear in court, but it was a horrible way to live, always looking in my rearview mirror.

* * * * *

Even as I write these words, I cannot begin to impress upon you the anguish I was feeling because I missed Logan so much. It killed me to become an every-other weekend father. Many times, I would drive up and down the street hoping to get a glimpse of my son playing outside.

I remember around this time, I leased a 2002 BMW coupe. One night I had been drinking and, for some reason I had been smoking a little grass as well. I was driving in the rain totally out of my mind. Between the grass and the booze, it made me frantic. I decided to drive by the house; it was around midnight. The roads were wet, and the side streets were winding. I hit the brakes and skidded out of control. The car did a 360 and slammed into the back of a tree, which put a huge V-shaped dent in the back of my trunk. I was pretty shook up, but not enough to stop me from finishing my quest. I drove by the house, parked across the street, and climbed atop a tree where I sat for a good hour or so, playing detective. It hadn't been the first time that I did a "drive-by."

I once shared that story with Tommy Smothers, one half of the Smothers Brothers. He commented, "I thought I was the only one in the world who did that. You had the same experience that I did with one of my ex-wives." God save us all.

When we finally went to court for our divorce, Asa and I never once looked at each other during the proceedings. Talk about a dagger through the heart!

That day after court, Jim Cantalin and I walked across the street to a local bar and drank for the rest of the afternoon. We were both big boozers, but I couldn't imagine him at that moment being more depressed than me. That afternoon in the bar, I told myself, *I've got to get out of Hollywood.*

Asa and I decided that we would sell the house and divide the money and everything in our checking and savings account. Luckily for me, Asa was very much a feminist and didn't want alimony, but she did take the child support that I insisted upon.

So much has been written about women going through divorce, but what about men? Men go through just as much pain as women do. I certainly did. I was in such a depressed state that I even considered suicide. Sleeping pills and champagne would have been the logical choice at the time if I wanted to take my life. It was the most painless way I could think of, and they were readily available to me. The only reason I didn't do anything drastic was because of my love for Logan. I didn't want him to grow up without a father.

After I got sober, I learned suicide is a permanent solution to a temporary problem.

That's probably why, twenty-five years later, I haven't remarried. I may have another marriage in me, but I definitely don't have the capacity for another divorce. I don't ever want to even think about another divorce.

* * * * *

Following the loss of my family, and needing a change of pace, a change of lifestyle, and a change of luck, I decided to pack my bags and head for London as an escape.

Ever since I was a little kid with my head buried in a geography book, it had always been a fantasy of mine to live in London. It remains to this day my favorite city.

London was not a bad place to be in 1971. There was a vast amount of wealth there, and the people always seemed so kind. And best of all, I could find work there as an actor on a regular basis. I might have even been more well-known as Kookie than in the States. As I've mentioned before, *77 Sunset Strip* was extremely popular in England.

I wasn't very popular though with a Mr. Ronald Shedlo. Ron was a movie producer in England and an old friend from back home. Ron came to our house almost every night for dinner when I was married to Asa. He was a nice enough guy, liked to dish the dirt, gossip, and tell stories about the industry.

Even though he came to dinner to our house countless times, he never once thought to bring a bottle of wine or flowers for Asa. He was a taker. Now living in England, I heard of a movie Ron was producing, and I called him to ask for a job. The fellow did mooch a few meals off me in his day. It was quid-pro-quo time.

"Hi, Ron, Edd Byrnes."

"Hi, Edd, it's great to hear from you. Where are you?"

"I'm in town. I live here now."

"Great, we must get together and have lunch."

"Well, the reason why I called is that there's a part in your new movie and I think I'd be perfect for it. Let's talk about it over lunch."

Without a second's hesitation, he told me, "No, Edd, you're not right for it."

Shocked and hurt, I took off the gloves and minced no words, "Ron, you practically lived off me for years. You never once brought a bottle of wine, you never brought flowers, nothing. Don't you think you owe me something for chrissakes?"

Coldly, he uttered one word, "No."

I guess that meant we were no longer on for lunch.

Though I would find work easily enough in London, I never got over Ron Shedlo's lack of loyalty in my time of need.

The "Swinging Sixties" in London had spilled over into the new decade. When I arrived, Tramps was the hottest discotheque in town. It was Laurence Harvey who introduced me to the owner, Johnny Gold, and after that meeting, I was a VIP member.

I practically lived at Tramps and met a lot of people whom I consider good friends to this day. My first night there I was seated next to this beautiful blonde named Sara, who was in her late twenties. We started talking. Sara had an English accent, which I must admit is a real turnon for me. I then asked her to dance, and we strutted our stuff for close to thirty minutes straight.

When we finished, a gentleman was waiting for her at a table.

"Edd, this is my husband, Basil." Major disappointment.

Sara and Basil became my instant friends. They were a young, vivacious, and good-looking couple, both hailing from wealthy English families. They owned a home in Hampstead Heath just outside of London. Along with Sara and Basil, I met others at the club, and we became a close-knit group who danced, mingled, and dined almost every night, and of course, the all important Sunday brunch out in the country finished off the week rather nicely.

Some of my other friends were Allan and Zoe Sutherland; Leonard Phillips and his wife; Monte Wolpe; and tennis players, Cliff Drysdale and Ray Moore.

These people were basically my family then, and we all became very close. Once you make a friend with the British, you make a friend for life. It takes an American a little longer to be accepted. Most Americans are more open initially. The British seem to want you to earn their friendship. I think it's a good way to develop lasting relationships.

I was staying in a hotel for the first few weeks in London until Sara announced, "Edd, you've got to find your own place here. This hotel is so expensive." She agreed to help me find a flat of my own.

One thing led to another, and Sara and I began having an affair. We were terribly attracted to each other and slept with each other steadily for a couple of months until I called it off.

"Sara, I don't think I can do this any longer. Basil's such a nice guy. I don't want to hurt his feelings or break up your marriage." We weren't in love with each other, and so we broke it off with Basil never knowing. To this day, he has no idea we had an affair. Looking back, I feel an enormous amount of guilt over this incident. It's quite typical of people with my background to want what others have. I've not had an affair with a married woman since.

In London, the night life starts hopping around 9:00 P.M. We'd gather for dinner and drinks, then end up at Tramps for dancing, more drinking, and come-what-may afterward. I'd get home at around 3:00 A.M. and not wake up until 5:00 P.M., whereupon I'd make some calls, see where everyone was getting together, and the process would start all over again. It was a party that seemed endless. The only alteration in the routine would be, providence willing, when I picked up some work, which I would then have to squeeze into my social schedule.

I was never really into the drug scene, even in Hollywood. I liked my wine too much to pay much attention to pharmaceuticals, but that all changed in London. My friend Bob, an extremely successful director of television commercials, gave me my first "snort" one night while I was staying in his penthouse apartment.

It was around 10:00 P.M., and I had worked all through that day and was feeling tired. I wanted to take a break from my normal routine and call it an early night. Bob wanted to go to Tramps. I objected. "Bob, I had to get up early today, I've been drinking, and it's too late." I had been burning the candle at both ends for days on end, and this was the night for my much-needed rest.

Bob was confident that in a few minutes I would be a new man. "Hey, don't worry, I'll get you up for this." He brought out a little tray of white powder complete with a straw.

"Is that cocaine?" I asked.

"Yeah, have you ever had it?" asked the director.

"No."

"Well, lean down, take two lines up each nostril and after that, believe me, you'll want to go to Tramps."

I did what the good director told me and took the required two hits in each nostril. Only about ten seconds elapsed before it hit me. All of a sudden, I felt like Superman. I was awake and rarin' to go.

We zipped on over to Tramps. I danced as fast as I could and drank until I started coming down again. Bob, sensing my lethargy, quickly broke out his trusty vial of the magical white powder, and I had a couple more snorts, which led to a few more drinks. About an hour later, we repeated the ritual. Cocaine is an "up and down" drug, unlike liquor, where I could keep a buzz going all night.

I also discovered LSD during my stay in England, but it wasn't a voluntary decision on my part to indulge in this most hallucinogenic drug.

On a Saturday afternoon, Sara, Basil, and I lunched at a favorite restaurant of ours called Trattoria's, where a lot of the acting world in London dined. I met a gorgeous young lady from Scandinavia named Tina. We got chummy right away, and I asked her if she would like to be my date for a wedding I was going to attend the next day. She said she'd love to.

I picked up Tina, and we drove over to Sara and Basil's in Hampstead Heath where we decided we would all ride together in Basil's Jaguar. The wedding was to take place out in the country approximately ninety miles from London.

It was a beautiful garden wedding, and at the reception, Tina struck up a conversation with someone, so Sara and I went for a walk along the road, where we came upon an enchanting old mansion. There was music coming from the building, and the door was open, so we peeked in, hoping to get a tour of the grounds. The people inside were very friendly, and they asked us in.

A gentleman named Thom King, who later became a producer, invited us upstairs for a rather unusual offering of delectables. It was the only time I had ever seen a buffet table of hashish. "This is from India," he said, "and this is from Pakistan," going right down the line. There were maybe five types of hashish on that table and by the looks of it, all quite potent.

"No thanks," I raised my hand, "I think I'll stick with the wine."

Sara and I went back downstairs and sat on a big comfortable sofa. On a table next to me was a plate of brownies. I picked one up to put into my mouth. Sara, not saying a word, grabbed my hand and prevented me from sinking my teeth into this mouth-watering goodie.

"What are you doing?" I asked her.

"Edd, you don't know what's in those brownies," Sara warned.

"Oh, come on, Sara. They're fine. The real stuff is upstairs, remember?"

"You don't know that for sure," she responded, ever the surrogate mother.

Waving off her womanly instincts, I downed the brownie in three bites. The damn thing was so tasty, it deserved a repeat performance, and I ate another one.

I dusted off the crumbs, sat up, and thanked our wonderful hosts for a splendid time. We walked back to the reception. By the time Sara and I caught up with Basil and Tina, it was already quite late. We decided to drive back to London as it was nearing midnight.

Basil was probably as drunk as I'd ever seen him, drinking white wine and champagne all day, and certainly was in no condition to drive. Sara was fine but was getting tired, so I offered to drive and let Sara and Basil sleep on the way back. Basil wouldn't hear of it. It was his Jaguar (men are very territorial about their cars), and he insisted on getting behind the wheel.

The country roads were very winding and not lit at all. Add to this Basil's breakneck speed and less-than-sober ability, and the drive was an experience in sheer terror.

I had never yelled at him before, but I did raise my voice: "Basil, slow the hell down, will ya?!"

Tina had a small scar on her face and when I first met her, I asked her how she got it. She told me that her boyfriend had hit another car while driving, and she had flown through the windshield. Tina had required a lot of plastic surgery, but still considered herself a very lucky girl. Knowing this, I wanted Basil to be especially careful.

I gave him a few more minutes to slow down, but he didn't heed my advice. Tina clutched my hand tightly and whispered into my ear, "Basil's too drunk to drive. He's really scaring me."

I thought that if I struck up a conversation with Basil, he might slow down and pay attention more to the road. By this time, Sara was dozing off, but before she did, I asked her to put on her safety belt, and she complied with my request. I didn't want the same thing that had happened to Tina to happen to Sara, or for that matter, to any of us in the car.

Basil maintained his reckless speed, and I was certain that it was only a matter of time before we crashed. I saw that Tina was biting her nails, so I knew I had to act fast.

"Will you pull over the car for a second, Basil? I have to relieve myself," I asked casually, then I begged, doubling over, acting as if I really had to go.

Finally, he pulled over, and Tina and I got out.

Basil begged and pleaded for us to get back in, but I told him, "We're not getting back in the car with you at the wheel."

"Eddie, don't be so silly. I'm OK."

"No, Basil, you're not OK. We'll find another ride home. Don't worry about us."

He pleaded one last time, and then he got mad and pressed the accelerator to the floor, spewing rocks about the road as he took off in a huff.

Tina said to me, "Thank God we're out of there. I just had the most eerie feeling that had we stayed in that car, we were going to get into an accident."

Ditto to that. I had the strongest premonition that had Tina and I stayed in that Jaguar, we would have crashed into a tree or an oncoming car. However, I knew that once we got out, Basil and Sara would get home safely, and they did. It was an overwhelming feeling of doom, and I would have done anything to get out of that vehicle.

Tina and I found ourselves in the middle of nowhere, and worse yet, it was getting cold. I gave Tina my jacket because she was wearing just a little sundress. I was wearing a silk shirt, and I began to feel the biting cold of the British weather.

We walked down this dark country road, with the shivering cold at our backs, clinging to each other. Just when I thought it couldn't get any worse, remember those two delicious brownies I scarfed down at the mansion? *Yeah, those two brownies!* As we started to walk, the brownies started to kick in.

I turned to this already petrified young lady and asked her, "You're trying to set me up, aren't you?"

"What?" she exclaimed, not believing what she just heard.

I gladly repeated for her what I had just said. "Admit it, you're trying to set me up."

"Edd, what are you talking about?" she asked in a pleading tone. Then she thought about what had transpired that evening. "Didn't you say that you ate some brownies at that mansion?" I had told her about the visit to the mansion, and she was piecing it all together. "There was probably some hash in those brownies. You're really getting strange on me, Edd. Are you all right?"

I didn't answer her question. As a matter of fact, I got a little bit more hostile, "YOU BITCH!" I now yelled. "YOU'RE TRYING TO SET ME UP!"

I had this strange fantasy that just down the road, Tina had arranged for eight guys to wait in some bushes, string me up, and beat the hell out of me. As crazy as it sounded, the vision was vividly real.

I found out later that these weren't just your average ordinary good ol'-fashioned hash brownies oven-baked by grandma. No sir. These were brownies laced with LSD. I was experiencing an acid trip.

Still believing she was part of a conspiracy, I pushed her away from me and ran down the road at full speed. As I was getting further and further away, I could hear her beg, "Edd, please come back. Don't do this. It's the brownies."

All of a sudden, there were headlights blinding my vision, and a car was coming straight for me. I dove to the side of the road without even thinking and rolled into a ditch with high weeds. Tina must have seen me dive, but she couldn't see me in the weeds. "Edd, are you all right?" she asked.

The car didn't stop, even for Tina. I wouldn't have either if I saw a madman in the middle of the road having an acid trip. My date, knowing I was in the weeds, pleaded with me to come out and stay with her. "Edd, come out. You're on acid. You're going to get killed if you stay out here."

She must have stood on that road begging me to come out for an hour, but I just listened quietly, eying her with suspicion, knowing she was out to set me up.

Finally, realizing she wasn't going to get me out of those weeds, she said aloud, "Edd, I'm going back to London. When I find help, I'll come back for you."

After she left, I crawled away on all fours deeper into the weeds, and finally it hit me, *I'm a Leo.* I was born on July 30, and Leo is my astrological sign, so all of a sudden, I'm on all fours, I'm a Leo, so it only made sense that I would act like a lion. I crawled around on all fours in the weeds, protecting my territory, and behaving like a lion. I didn't feel drunk or high, I just felt like the King of the Jungle. I stayed in that frame of mind for five very long hours.

When the sun came up and the acid wore off, I felt like Dr. David Bruce Banner after he awoke from the transformation of the Incredible Hulk.

When I was able to put together the events of the previous night, it hit me, *Oh my God, what happened to Tina? Those damn brownies—I'm going to kill that host!*

As I was walking down the road, I spotted a bus that had a sign on top that read "Edinburgh/London." I flagged down the bus, and as I got on board, the driver asked with typical wry British humor, "Have a rough night, mate?" I looked down and discovered I was covered with mud and dried dirt. I was more than disheveled, I was a mess.

Luckily, I had a few pounds in my pocket, enough to get me by bus to Victoria Station and then by cab back to my flat. I fell into bed and slept for twelve hours straight. When I got up, I called Tina to see if she was okay.

"Thank God you're all right." She sounded happy to hear my voice.

"Yeah, I'm OK. Are you doing fine? How was your trip back?"

"I made it back, but can we meet for coffee?" she asked.

We met, and her story was much more terrifying than my experience. She told me that after she left me in the weeds, about a half mile down the road, a truck with two men in the cab pulled over to give her a lift.

About a mile into the trip, she had this feeling they were planning to rape her. "I could just tell by the way they were touching me, putting their hands on my legs, dropping sexual innuendos that they had plans of their own. They were definitely going to rape me, if not kill me," she stated, her voice choking up.

"Then I started turning the table on them. I knew that if I kept talking, something would happen to make them think twice. I told them that they reminded me of my brothers and how protected and safe I felt with them." By then, Tina could see shame in their eyes, and they ended up driving her all the way to a train station that would take her back to London, even lending her the fare to get back home. Tina was no dummy.

Despite my harrowing experience with the LSD, I continued to drink, use cocaine, and party hard while in London. They say old habits die hard, and this was only the beginning of a twelve-year run of substance abuse. The sad thing about alcohol versus drugs, it just takes a little longer to kill you.

CHAPTER THIRTEEN

The Great Escape

I WAS JET-SETTING back and forth between London and the United States either for work or to see Logan. Ever since Logan was five, he'd had his own phone. When I was in London, I wanted to have a direct connection to him as opposed to calling and having Asa answer. Her voice would only bring me pain. Eventually, I crossed the pond for some serious therapy; at the time, I considered England my home.

Despite my constant abuse of alcohol and its numbing effect, I was becoming increasingly hostile toward Asa, blaming her for the breakup of our marriage. My rage got so out of control that I had thoughts of killing her. I knew that I could never go through with it, simply because I didn't want Logan to grow up without a mother. Nonetheless, I can now understand the anger and the urge to kill either one's ex-spouse or any person. I was definitely there on the edge for a while.

At one point in London, I stayed with a couple that Asa and I had known from Hutton Drive, David and Brigid Hedison. David was a fellow television actor who starred in *Voyage to the Bottom of the Sea.* He also toured with me in a play called *Under the Yum Yum Tree* for three months around the United States. We became really good friends.

Before one of the performances, David and I went out for dinner and had quite a few drinks. On stage that night, David picked up the wrong cue and dropped about eight pages of dialogue. The curtain usually came down at 10:20. On that night, we ended around 10:00. I'm sure a few members of the audience went home, scratching their heads.

When David left the play, Tab Hunter took his place. Tab never got the laughs that David did. I'd tell Tab, "Do you want to know how to get a really big laugh out of this line?"

But Tab would cut me short. "David had his way of doing things, and I have my way." The play suffered severely when Tab Hunter took over David's role.

One of the first nights I was at the Hedison's, I was in such torment that I began to cry. And cry. And I couldn't stop crying. I cried out so loudly, the effect was that of a wounded animal. I was actually howling when David came in to talk to me. He found me on the floor in his guestroom, curled up in the fetal position.

By that next morning, my eyes were bloodshot, and my face had blown up like a balloon. It looked as if I were in a prize fight and I came out the worse for wear.

Although I didn't know it then, I was going through a mourning period as though I'd lost a loved one who had died. Of course, Logan was involved, too. I knew I needed help, and I decided, after much thought and research, to try Gestalt therapy when I was back in California.

In Gestalt therapy, they wanted to know what I was feeling at the moment. They weren't interested in talking about the past. They weren't interested in the future. They were interested in *right now.*

My therapist, Eric Marcus, MD, suggested group therapy as opposed to one-on-one counseling to deal with my anger. In that group, there would be several other people going through the same thing as me, and we could become a support system for each other.

The main thrust of the therapy would be to act out and deal with our feelings through role-playing. I was one of a group of eight, and we'd start the session with our shoes off, seated on the floor with big fluffy pillows. The objective was to be in a comfortable environment while dealing with our various individual, yet similar, feelings.

One weekend, we had a retreat up in Crestline, California, a few miles south of Lake Arrowhead. Eric and his assistant, Dorothy, were conducting an "Anger Workshop," and I signed up to go with a young lady who I was seeing at the time. There were twelve other couples present, and there was a lot of crying, yelling, and screaming.

What Eric had me do, because he knew of my past history, was to place myself into a woman's arms and have her hold me like a newborn child. He even went so far as to have me suck on a baby bottle filled with warm water and honey while this woman rocked me in her arms. She'd say things like, "I love you. You're the cutest little baby in the whole wide world." Or she might sing to me, "Rock-a-bye-baby on the treetop." The basic emotion was to feel love at a young age when my mother was feeding me. I had a hard time playing this role. I kept laughing, and of course, I insisted that I was breast-fed as a child.

Another task was to strip down nude and have two women and two men massage me, my head, temples, chest, arms, legs and down to my feet. I had a very hard time having this done to me, and then Eric told me, "Just accept this love, Edd." After the first ten minutes, I did begin to relax. After the massage, the four held their hands, put me in the center, and rocked me back and forth. It was really a beautiful weekend, and I was on a natural high for three days afterwards.

When our group got back to Los Angeles, I was encouraged to act out my anger while a female member of our group played the role of Asa. If I really wanted to kill off Asa, Eric told me, to make the pain go away, I'd have to act it out. I would really have to get in touch with my feelings.

Eric encouraged me to put my hands around "Asa's" throat as though I were strangling her and killing her off. I did this by looking into this woman's eyes and strangling a pillow that was lying on her neck.

I then vented my anger, "YOU BITCH! YOU FUCKING BITCH! WHY DID YOU HURT ME SO MUCH? WHY DID YOU LEAVE ME? WHY DIDN'T YOU TRY AND WORK IT OUT? WHY DID YOU BREAK UP OUR FAMILY?"

I was also letting the anger out I had toward my mother. "Why didn't she make her marriage work? Why did I have to grow up without a family? Why couldn't she keep the family together? The bitch . . ."

After shouting my hostilities, the pent-up anger left my body temporarily. There were many days where I had to repeat this process when the rage consumed me again.

Now, I'm sure that many of you disagree with this method, but I must defend it. Many times the thought to kill my wife would leave me for a few weeks, and when it came back, I'd return to therapy and work it out through role-playing. There is no doubt this was a highly controversial method. Rather than fantasizing killing Asa, isn't it better to act it out in a more positive, and certainly less permanent and criminal manner?

Asa knew that I was angry with her, but I don't think she ever realized the full extent of it. Once, while driving with her in Beverly Hills, we started to argue. I raised my hand and had the urge to smack her. There must have been a look in my eyes that scared her enough so that she jumped out of the car, which was probably a smart thing to do in that situation. No matter how I may have felt, I never physically beat her. However, there was no denying I was filled with hostility toward this woman. I desperately needed some help to deal with the rage dwelling inside of me.

Also through Gestalt therapy, I discovered I still harbored a deep-seated resentment toward my father, and Eric felt that I should act out that as well.

How does a man resolve an issue with a father who's been dead for more than twenty-five years?

"You have to forgive him," Eric told me softly. "You have to say good-bye to your father *and* forgive him."

In therapy, in the presence of others, we held a mock funeral, and I had to go up to my father's open casket and tell him that I forgave him. It wasn't an easy thing to do.

It went something like this: "Pop, I realize that I've been as mad as hell at you ever since you came back from the war. I realize you did the best that you could do under the circumstances, and I forgive you for not being the father that I felt you should have been."

I then broke down and cried real tears for him. Twenty-five years of carrying around this garbage in the pit of my stomach had been released. It helped immensely to get rid of that poison in my system so that I could get on with the rest of my life. I was still quite young, only thirty-five, and I would be forever grateful to Eric Marcus and Gestalt therapy for helping me in one of my darkest hours. However, alcohol was still my best friend, but slowly it was becoming my worst enemy.

* * * * *

Stardust is probably the movie I am proudest to have been associated with, but oddly enough, I was never satisfied with my performance.

The movie was based loosely on the story of the Beatles, but chose to utilize literary license and call the foursome "The Stray Cats."

This movie has attained cult status in the United States and is considered a classic in Britain.

The film was a sequel to *That'll Be the Day,* starring David Essex.

I was seeing producer David Puttnam's secretary, and she told me, "David's getting ready to make this film over here and there's a part in it for an American TV reporter. I think you'd be great." Nothing is more helpful than inside information.

My friend suggested to Mr. Puttnam that Edd Byrnes was very interested in being in his film.

"You think so?" he asked quizzically.

"I think I can get him to do it," she said with an air of confidence.

I was in Dallas doing a play when I got a call at my hotel.

"Edd Byrnes?"

"Speaking."

"David Puttnam here."

Acting as if I didn't know what was going on, I put on my most charming voice, "David, hi, it's really good to hear from you."

"Linda's been telling me you want to be in this movie. There are two parts here for American reporters, but they're both so minuscule, I don't want to insult you by offering them to you. I've been thinking, and I've decided to merge the two parts into one. Do you think you might still be interested?"

"That will be fine," I assured him.

While I was doing *Ready When You Are, C. B.* at Granny's Dinner Theater in Dallas, a woman in her twenties had come backstage. After the usual pleasantries, I asked her to dinner and drinks. We went back to my hotel and ended up making love. As we got dressed, the woman had some startling news for me.

"Edd, I have a confession to make," my new lover said quietly.

"What is it?"

She boldly stated, "I've been stalking you for three years."

"What do you mean by *stalking* me for the past three years?"

"Well, I've been attracted to you for quite some time, and I've been following you for the past three years, trying to find out where I could meet you."

My stalker had been quickly shown the door, and I never saw her again. Unfortunately, my Oldsmobile did. When I went down for it the next morning in the hotel garage, it looked as if someone had taken a baseball bat and used it for batting practice. When I hung up the phone with David Puttnam that day, I was doubly glad to be working in my favorite city again, presumably away from my stalking admirer's path.

Stardust was one of those magical films where all of the pieces of the puzzle fit and everything just falls in line. The picture featured several fine actors, including Larry Hagman, David Essex, Adam Faith, and rocker Keith Moon.

The director, Michael Apted, directed several television commercials before his debut with *The Triple Echo*. This movie would be his second feature film, and it didn't take me long to figure out this guy was going to be in the major leagues one day. So far, he has proven me right. He went on to direct such hits as *Coal Miner's Daughter, Gorillas in the Mist, Class Action*, and *Thunderheart*. He is a proven talent.

I had known Larry Hagman previously but never had the opportunity to work with him. Our other location was in Gaudix, Spain, where we were to shoot in and around a castle. The whole crew and cast stayed in the only hotel in town. While we weren't working, Larry would go down to Morocco and bring back some of the finest hash I had ever ingested. However, it was extremely dangerous to smuggle contraband into Spain, and I asked Larry, "Do you know what happens if you get caught with this stuff?" I didn't even let him answer, "They don't lock you up and throw away the key. They lock you up and let you rot!"

I should know. I had a run in of my own with the Spanish police in Almeria while I was starring in a film called *The Killing Ground*. Every day, the desk clerk would give me a wake-up call at 6:00 A.M. sharp. One day when I wasn't working, the clerk kept calling to wake me up. I personally didn't mind his incessant ringing, but Logan was a baby at the time. The calls interrupted his sleep, and in seconds, he would be crying.

Exasperated, I went downstairs to the front-desk clerk, grabbed him, and shook him by the lapels. "Don't wake me up anymore. I'm not working today." Then I went back to bed. About twenty minutes later, the police were pounding on my door and "Mr. Wake-up Call" was pointing at me and telling them in Spanish I was the bad boy who had the audacity to grab and shake him like a martini.

The police put me in the car and hauled me off to the local police station. Asa called the actor James Franciscus, who happened to be staying in our hotel, and he came to my rescue. I don't know what Jim said or did, but he kept me from being thrown in jail.

Now, Larry Hagman was smuggling in this exquisite hash, and I was getting visions of Turkish prisons, foreign-speaking men, who took showers once a week, knifing me in the abdominal cavity when I wasn't looking, basically what Brad Davis had experienced in *Midnight Express.*

Larry wasn't too concerned, "Just don't worry about it, Edd," he calmly told me.

Mr. Hagman is a very funny man, and he has this peculiar habit where he doesn't speak at all on Sundays. Why? I don't know, but he had a few strange quirks that I didn't fully understand. He didn't perform that ritual on this film, but he's famous in town for it now. He's a really good guy, and I was very happy for him when he became enormously popular as J. R. Ewing on *Dallas* just a few years later. (If you watch *Stardust,* you'll notice that Larry was playing an early version of J. R. Ewing. It was exactly the same character.) Had we been caught with that hashish in Spain, I doubt that even J. R. Ewing could have bribed the right politicians to get us out of jail.

During the day, we'd shoot at this wonderful old castle with a break for an exotic lunch. There was always plenty of red and white wine with our meals, and I enjoyed the experience very much. The biggest problem now, of course, is that I just don't remember very many of these enjoyable moments of my life.

I do remember, though, a very treacherous afternoon when I had to go up in a helicopter under "less than desirable" conditions. First, let me state emphatically that I *hate* being a passenger in a helicopter. On that day, I was required to get out of the helicopter, run across the roof of the castle, and report on the scene. I had already performed the routine twice, and this white-knuckled passenger couldn't bear the thought of a third rendition.

Michael Apted wanted one more shot, and the pilot protested claiming that the weather was too choppy. The weather was hideously windy at best on the second try, and it was getting worse by the minute. Let me add that while I was in the chopper, the assistant cameraman who worked on *Dr. Zhivago,* was on board. He announced, "Yeah, I worked with David Lean on *Dr. Zhivago* when the helicopter crashed. Mr. Lean wanted one more shot, but the pilot didn't want to. The copter crashed, killing the cinematographer and the pilot."

Was this guy trying to tell me something? Did I need to hear this bit of film trivia? Thank God nothing happened to us on the third try, and Michael Apted was quite happy with the shot. This was good, because there was not going to be a fourth take. Not that day.

My big scene took place with David Essex, who played a John Lennon-like character. Essex was to be dressed in a white suit throughout the movie, and I said to him, "You know what would really go great with that white suit? Why don't you get a red rose and put it in your coat lapel? Why, you'll really look like a rock star!" He took my advice.

In the scene, I was interviewing David Essex who was becoming a big rock star in the film. As I was asking him questions, he has an overdose right in front of me.

David Essex's character shot up with heroin immediately before our interview, and he passed out. The ambulance arrived and whisked him away with the back doors shut, thus ending the movie.

The film was gritty, real, improvisational, and I knew it was going to be something special. Out of all of the performances I had ever given, it was the one I liked least. My character in the movie, strangely enough called Edd Byrnes, had very little energy. Perhaps it was because I had become a daily drinker.

When I finished filming *Stardust,* I headed straight for the Marbella Beach Club, an international club for the wealthy and famous. While poolside at the club one day, I met this wonderful girl from Amsterdam. She was all of twenty years old, a part-time model and student, and Jeremy Lloyd from *Laugh-In* was chatting her up. I looked straight at this girl, and my heart just stopped. Jeremy Lloyd became part of the background as she became the target of my finely tuned tunnel vision. Her name was Brecken.

I took Brecken out, and while at a party, she whispered ever so softly in my ear, "Don't make me fall in love with you." From that first day, Brecken and I were inseparable. We would make love five times a day: at daybreak, after lunch, after a siesta, before we went out, and before we went to bed. This excursion continued for ten days straight. I don't think I could do that now (well, maybe only three times a day—yeah Eddie, sure).

It was a perfect ten days with a beautiful woman and not a care in the world. Brecken's nickname for me was "Bastard" because she would always say to me, "You're going to ruin my life, you bastard." We never had an argument, and we'd go out to lunch, swim, take drives to other villages in the mountains, and attend wonderful parties and discos in Marbella. Oh, and I almost forgot, we drank *a lot* of wine.

When our ten days were up, I couldn't stand to leave this sweet little angel. I asked her to come back with me to London to extend our time together. Brecken was studying to be a doctor and knew that if she went with me to London, we'd end up genuinely falling in love, and maybe getting married. That would have put a halt to both our plans.

"If I don't go now, you'll ruin my life, you bastard," she teased me, but I could tell she might have meant it to be serious as well.

I told my new sweetheart, "I'm so crazy about you, I can't leave you." I had to be back in London for the looping of *Stardust,* and I was quite truthful with the production assistant over the phone. "Look, I met this wonderful person, and I want to spend the rest of the week with her. Is it all right for me to come in a week later to do the looping?"

"That's fine, Edd. Enjoy," was the reply. Love those Brits.

It was probably the most passionate affair with a woman I've ever experienced. I was in love for ten days, but I felt that there would always be someone to take Brecken's place. In a sweet way, in mine or anyone's life, it's like little snowflakes of memories. I obviously never forgot Brecken, and I'll always have those ten days of euphoric memories in Marbella.

I have always loved European women. They just seem to be more attentive to a man. They're not afraid to be women. They play fewer games and are more direct than American women. They don't want to have the balls in the relationship. There's a therapist in Los Angeles by the name of Pat Allen who hit the nail right on the head when she said in one of her seminars, "Now ladies, when you go home to your husband or boyfriends from work tonight, don't forget to leave your balls in your desk drawer." That's a woman therapist giving the advice, not Edd Byrnes.

* * * * *

I had been crisscrossing the Atlantic for almost four years when I decided to return to the United States. I needed to get back, mainly because I missed Logan so much. When I was in England, Logan would visit me. He'd arrive on the plane escorted by a stewardess, and we'd hug ever so tightly. I wanted so much to be there for him, but I was leading this totally double life. The life I was leading in London had nothing to do with reality, so I went home.

During this period, I was into what I term my "drinking and driving" phase. I rented a house in Los Angeles on Sherbourne Drive. Every Tuesday it became a ritual for me to drive down to Newport Beach and spend the day.

I would start by drinking in the morning before packing an ice chest with five bottles of wine in case I ran out. Corkscrews were strewn about the car. I liked to drink my two-dollar-a-bottle Wente Brothers Chablis in an antique silver goblet. That was very kingly to me, to drink out of an expensive silver goblet. That's how the alcoholic thinks. How could I possibly have a drinking problem if I'm sipping out of a silver goblet that belongs in a museum?

I'd usually have lunch at Josh Slocum's, a restaurant right on Pacific Coast Highway, with a splendid view of the marina. I'd sit at a table, sipping my wine. After my meal, I'd hit a couple of the local watering holes and drink well into the night. I became a regular.

I met this beautiful blonde girl named Lorraine (I call them "girls" because that's what they were, usually in their early twenties), and we struck up a casual conversation over drinks.

Lorraine became my cocaine connection when I needed a "lift" to pick me up out of my alcoholic daze. Now I was high, drunk, and worst of all, driving a four-thousand-pound vehicle, itself a potentially lethal weapon, back to Los Angeles.

After a few weeks, Lorraine graduated to being my cocaine dealer/lover and would spend the weekends with me in my house in L.A. She'd call me on a Friday and ask, "How much cocaine should

I bring up for tonight?" and I'd tell her, "Around $300 worth." Then, as now, cocaine is an extremely expensive habit. Anybody who knows anything about the drug knows that $300 worth is not a whole lot, but it'll do the trick. You can go through that much in about a half-hour.

Before Lorraine would leave Newport Beach, she'd ask me, "Now, we're going to go out tonight, right, Edd?" I'd ease her fears. "Of course. We'll go for dinner, a movie, and maybe go dancing," and she'd be happy.

At least, that was the idea before I'd take a hit of the coke. I got into this pattern of her coming to my house, snorting the coke, having sex, drinking wine, taking some sleeping pills, and passing out.

Once the coke went up my nose, so did our plans for the evening. When you have cocaine, there's nothing else out there. It's all there in front of your face. Why would I leave, especially when I have a beautiful woman? Why would I want to go out? I had my cocaine, I had my champagne, I had my woman, I had my wine, food, a beautiful home, a king-sized bed, movies, and my two beloved Akitas that Asa could never take away from me again. I had it all right there in my house.

There's no reason to get in the car and drive to a restaurant. Coke kills the appetite. It's the greatest drug in the world for losing weight. It also kills the appetite to do anything else when all you want to do is snort more of the powder.

After two months of this pattern every single weekend, she gave me the ultimatum, "Edd, I'm not coming up there again without set plans. Let's go out and have some fun!"

I responded, "I'm going to get us some theater tickets," and I really did. When Lorraine came up, I showed her the tickets and she got all excited. I put up, so now she had to. "Before we go out, let's do a few lines," I said. We did the lines and the next thing I remember is waking up the next morning, and the theater tickets were still on the table. After the cocaine wore off, I had to knock myself out with red wine because white wine always picked me up. I suffered from insomnia, mainly because I was still reeling from my divorce from Asa. I would usually awake around 4:00 A.M., and I'd have a glass of red wine on my nightstand and a sleeping pill to knock me out again.

Lorraine finally had enough of me. I called her that Friday and asked, "Are you coming up this weekend?" She replied, "Edd, you're trying to kill yourself. You drink all day, then I come up, you do some coke, then you drink more wine, then you take sleeping pills. I don't want to wake up one morning to discover your cold, dead body. I just cannot see you anymore." It's pretty sad when your own coke dealer cuts you off.

The same situation arose again with a woman I met in Texas named Rose. I had been flying her in on weekends and performing the same ritual, *sans* the cocaine.

My unusual behavior wore on Rose, and it grated upon her emotions as well. She told me the same exact thing, "I've gotta tell you Edd, I can't spend the weekend with you anymore. I'm going to wake up next to you and find you dead." She was serious, although at the time I thought she was being overdramatic. She had not gotten my attention.

It was a scary thought, but that's where the alcohol was taking me. What was even scarier was that I would continue to drink in this fashion for another seven years.

CHAPTER FOURTEEN

Amanda

OTHER THAN my role as Kookie on *77 Sunset Strip*, I'm known to a newer generation of fans as that crazy, hip-hopping, be-bopping, if not a tad bit lecherous, rock-and-roll television host of "National Bandstand," Vince Fontaine. This was, of course, in the 1978 film classic, *Grease*. (My role was originally offered to Dick Clark by producer Allan Carr, but Dick wanted too much money. Lucky for me!)

The play had been a hit on Broadway for several years and was one of the few films in recent history to live up to all of the hype, ballyhoo, and expectations of a major blockbuster film. To this date, *Grease* has grossed more than $400 million worldwide, and it is still listed as the most successful musical of all time.

I had never been in a movie where I had the luxury of five weeks of rehearsals. The choreographer, Pat Birch, insisted that I give her my individual best efforts for these full five weeks.

"But I only have one scene where I have to dance," I playfully objected.

The feisty choreographer told me, "Everyone on this picture is going to go through rehearsals for five weeks. We're all going to be one big, happy family."

Pat was right; it was like a family. Everyone had to rehearse together, yet even before that, we had to perform stretching exercises and calisthenics in the morning. Push-ups, sit-ups, jumping jacks, you name it, we did it. It obviously showed in the movie, and Pat Birch remains to this day one of the most talented ladies in the business. I will even go on record to say that she was the "unofficial" director of that movie. Randal Kleiser was the official director, but Pat was definitely the driving force behind the picture.

I couldn't really cry too much about the rehearsals and the exercises because I was surrounded by all of these beautiful dancers, and on top of that, they paid me a *very* generous salary.

At the end of the five weeks, we actually performed all of the numbers for the executives at Paramount from beginning to end. There was such a buzz surrounding the film, that all the stars on the lot came by to watch. I remember my old pal Jack Nicholson stopping by for a visit. Jack was filming *Goin' South*, and together we would watch the young dancers kick up their heels. That was one thing Jack and I would always have in common, a full appreciation for the opposite sex.

I was also able to incorporate some of my gymnastic skills into the final cut. Once I was practicing some handsprings and walking on my hands in between shots. Pat Birch saw me goofing around and came over to say, "Edd, I didn't know you could do that." She then added, "I want you to dive into the shot, perform a handspring, and then grab the microphone."

We shot the scene over a period of two weeks, and it worked out perfectly. I'm still amazed to this day that I was able to perform those feats at my age, and more to my current amazement, I did this while I was in the heavy phase of my drinking. I remember asking actress,

Dinah Manoff, who was in the movie, if everyone on the set knew I was drinking.

"Of course," came her reply. "You were sipping on your wine all day. It was no secret to anyone."

That's the funny thing about alcoholics, they think everyone around them is oblivious when in actuality, it's the drinker who can't see his own hand in front of his face.

OK, I'm sure all of you fellow "movie buffs" want to know what John Travolta and Olivia Newton-John are like, right?

John Travolta is probably one of the nicest guys ever to grace the silver screen. At that time in his career, he was the hottest star on the planet. He was an industry unto himself, and yet, he seemed to be handling stardom with relative ease. He did kind of quiz me on what it was like to be a teen idol and how I adjusted to the rigors of stardom. John was still involved with the television series *Welcome Back, Kotter.* I told him that since he was now a movie star, he should get out of the series as soon as possible. I told him, "The public will not pay to watch you in the movies if they can see you at home for free." I can only state simply that I liked John a lot and am thrilled for his comeback in *Pulp Fiction* and *Get Shorty.*

Olivia Newton-John was a very shy woman. Several times during the movie, she'd walk by, and I'd say, "Hi, Olivia," and she'd say "hello" back, but then she'd put her head down and walk away. She did this constantly, and we really never had what constituted a genuine conversation.

An interesting little sidebar to the film occurred when I flew back on one of my many trips to New York. I happened to be sitting next to Frankie Valli in the first-class section. He sang the title song for the *Grease* soundtrack and spent a full four hours on the one number. The soundtrack album sold a mint, and he collected more than a million dollars for his four hours worth of work. "It was the biggest payday of my life," he winked. My heart sank just a bit. If my rap over the titles of the movie had not been omitted from the album, I too might have had a million-dollar payday.

When I wasn't working, I was busy participating in celebrity/pro tennis tournaments where celebrities and professional tennis players are matched up together. It makes for one interesting game.

One of the first tournaments I played was in Chicago. Accommodations were made so that I would stay at the famous Drake Hotel. I met up with my sister, Jo-Ann, and we were put in the beautiful two-bedroom Presidential Suite.

After unpacking, we left for the tournament. When I got back to our suite, I found all our belongings had been moved into another room. I was told by hotel management that Billie Jean King and her girlfriend had been mistakenly taken to my suite first, then when it was obvious that someone was already occupying that room, she was taken to her correct suite. However, it was much smaller and less luxurious than mine.

Ms. King in those days was a King, or a female version of a six-hundred-pound gorilla. She made such a stink over her accommodations that the management gave in and moved my things into her smaller suite while she took over mine.

I wasn't that upset (more amused than anything) over the fact that this lady had bulldozed her way into my suite, but was amazed to think that she almost caused a riot over such a trivial thing.

Advantage, Ms. King.

After I finished work on *Grease*, I arranged a celebrity/pro tennis tournament in Maui, Hawaii, during the summer of 1978. I was putting together a list of my friends who played tennis, and this included, among others, Kirk Douglas, Lloyd Bridges, Adam West, Bill Cosby, and Desi Arnaz, Jr.

While at a luau, I saw a tall, brown-haired woman, clothed in a Hawaiian sundress cut above her knees, but my view was from the back. She was someone special already, and I wanted to see her face.

I went and introduced myself, and she told me her name was Amanda, and she was in Hawaii on vacation from Houston.

I discovered this beauty was a very good tennis player, and I invited her to the tournament the next day. I had a three-bedroom suite overlooking the ocean. I brought along Logan and my mother. She had never been to Hawaii, and I thought this was the perfect opportunity for her to see this most enchanting place.

After three wonderful days and nights of lunches, dinners, parties, and tennis, Amanda and I became lovers. She was extremely mature for her age and somehow I had it in my mind that she was in her early twenties.

"I'm only nineteen, Edd," said Amanda.

"That's OK," I gulped. "I'm only forty-five."

Despite our age difference, I was *very* attracted to this young lady from Houston. I was leaving for Los Angeles the next day, and, like the woman from Amsterdam, I just could not bear the thought of leaving this special person.

"Have you ever been to Los Angeles?" I asked her.

"No, but I've always wanted to go there." Her reply was all that I needed to hear.

"Well, why don't you come along for four or five days, and I'll take you to some of my favorite restaurants, and we'll play some tennis and take some drives up the coast."

Amanda stayed for five years.

At first, I thought she would stay perhaps five days and then return to Houston. I planned to fly her in on the weekends, but the more I got to know her, the more we became involved.

Amanda had only one year of college, and she was on summer break when she met me. She liked traveling the globe with this star from Hollywood, and she became my constant companion. She was my playmate, and not just in a sexual way. She was excellent company, and I was falling in love.

I educated her about wine, restaurants, and the good things in life, just as John Harjes did with me. We traveled that first year together to London, Mexico, back to Maui, and a few other exotic locations. We got along like a couple of clams at high tide, safe until the tide turned away. I'd always warn her, "One of these days I'm going to have to kick you out of the nest, and you're going to have to leave me."

After one full year of traveling, partying, and living together, I told Amanda that she might want to start thinking about a career. I gently suggested that "I don't think it's good for you to just hang out with me all of the time." She agreed and got a job for an oil company on Wilshire Boulevard as an administrative aide.

I finally felt that I was stable enough to bring Logan back into my life in a fairly permanent setting. I wanted a family and, with Asa's blessing, Logan came to live with me again. I even shelled out $500 and bought us a male Akita puppy, if only to round out the new family.

Very quickly friction developed between Amanda and Logan. They were only four years apart, and I'm sure Logan felt that she was trying to replace Asa. Amanda may have had a special place in my life, but she wasn't Logan's mother. If anything, she was more my nurse and confidante.

While I was with Amanda, I was in and out of hospitals with drinking bouts and pancreatic attacks. Everyone, and most especially actors, think that they'll be young and thin for the rest of their lives. What no one told me was that this lifestyle does eventually catch up to you. It was certainly catching up with me, but that didn't stop me from drinking my precious wine.

My credo was that I wouldn't drink while I was working because I really wanted to do a good job. At one point, I had wanted to lose some weight before I was to shoot a television movie, because the camera adds about ten pounds to your weight. I actually stopped drinking for two weeks and went to a diet doctor in Beverly Hills.

He prescribed diet pills and all of a sudden, I was losing the weight. On the flip side, I didn't have a bowel movement for several days. After *nine* days, I decided I needed to see another doctor. I checked into Cedars-Sinai Hospital. I don't want to go through the horrors of describing to you what they did to me, let it suffice to say that they had to drill "it" out of me. Bob Vila wouldn't have wanted to touch this one with a ten-foot pole.

The cost was three thousand dollars for a three-day stay. That was an expensive way to lose some weight. What I didn't know was that the alcohol was destroying certain bodily functions, and when one's body doesn't work properly, the whole system quite literally shuts down.

I also suffered severe pancreatic attacks for eight hours at a stretch.

Once, while I was working in England, at around ten at night, I got stomach pains. I knew it was only a matter of time before it became a full-fledged attack.

I was taken to St. George Hospital in London (which no longer exists) but still felt obligated to go to work the next day. I thought they might give me some pills, and I'd be on my way.

"Oh, no sir, we have to put you through all of the proper x-rays," I was told.

Despite my drinking, I had then (as I do now) prided myself on never missing a day's work, and I'd be damned if I was going to miss out even one day from the set. I wasn't given anything to numb the pain until they knew for sure what was wrong with me. Throughout the night, I was reeling in pain, and I begged, "Isn't there anything you can give me?" My plea was met with stony silence.

I was put into a ward with eighteen other people. I was in the fetal position in serious agony. I finally passed out from the pain and was awakened the next morning around six by an English gentleman singing, "Oh what a beautiful morning . . . "

What the hell kind of snake pit am I in? I wondered as I awoke.

A nurse finally came in asking, "Could I get you a cup of tea, love, perhaps a newspaper?"

"Actually, I'd like to get the hell out of here," I responded.

"Well, let's see what the doctors have to say."

The doctor came in and highly discouraged my leaving, but I still had my foolish pride. I couldn't miss that day's work. I went to the front desk to check out and asked for the bill.

"No charge, sir. We practice socialized medicine here."

"Even for an American?" I asked.

"Even for a Yank," he assured me.

I arranged for my driver to pick me up at a hotel down the street from the hospital. It was all that I could do to stand up. The driver couldn't help but notice that I was looking very pale and sickly.

I arrived on location and was told the same thing by some of the cast members, but I still hung on and made it through the day. It was a hell of a price to pay for my wine.

Amanda had to call several times for an ambulance while I was writhing in agony on the floor. When the bouts became more frequent, she gave up on the ambulance and drove me instead to the hospital. The attacks were so painful, I wouldn't wish them on my own worst enemy, maybe even a mother-in-law. Imagine doubling over in pain for almost half a day and not being able to do a thing about it. Now, imagine that I would still go out and drink after these attacks subsided. You would think that pain was still fresh in my memory, but the liquor was taking over my life, and suddenly I was on a train going not to New Orleans, but directly to Hell, and there wasn't any way to get off.

Why would this young girl who had so much on the ball stay with a man almost twenty-six years her senior and put up with his drinking? And her parents were not too thrilled that she was living with a so-called "Hollywood actor." She remained, quite simply, because she was still very young and impressionable. Had she been thirty instead of nineteen, the door would have probably hit me in the ass much sooner, to the sound of shattering glass.

* * * * *

In the 1950s, CBS aired a successful television series called *The Millionaire*, in which each week a lucky person was awarded a million dollars. The series plot attempted to show how each recipient adjusted to the sudden wealth. In 1979, Paramount updated the concept in a pilot called "$weepstake$," where I played a game-show host.

It was the easiest job I'd ever landed. Because the show was a three-story anthology, my character was only in about a third of the show. All of my lines were on cue cards, so I never had to memorize any dialogue. In addition, I worked from 8:00 A.M. to noon, and after that, I was done for the day. I was paid quite handsomely for my four hours of work. My salary was a princely sum of five thousand dollars a week. I never had it so good.

One day I got quite a shock. Remember that BMW that I wrecked (the trunk with the V-shape dent) way back in 1971 before I left for London? I never actually turned it in. I lent the car to a friend, asking him to turn it in two weeks when the lease expired. My friend also had an accident in the car, and he dropped it off in "less than mint" condition to the leasing company.

I had forgotten about the car years ago, but the leasing firm surely hadn't. On the set of "$weepstake$," I got a call from the payroll department and was told that the Sheriff's Department had picked up about thirty-seven hundred dollars of my paycheck.

"What?" I asked in amazement.

It seems that the leasing company had a lien and had been tracking me down for eight years. I had been on the cover of *TV Guide*, and the company now knew where to find me. I had been on the run ever since my divorce from Asa. They had finally caught up to me because with the pilot being picked up, I was going to be in one place for thirteen weeks.

A couple of days later I received a call from someone at the Department of Motor Vehicles.

"Hi, my name is Mark Smith, and I'm a big fan of yours. I have a file on you from this leasing company regarding the crashed BMW. I thought maybe we could meet for lunch, and I could show you the file."

When I met the gentleman, he pulled out a file, maybe six inches thick. The leasing company had been hunting me for years, spending a fortune trying to find me, including hiring detectives. As I was reading the file, I began to feel like Dr. Richard Kimble from *The Fugitive.*

$weepstake$ featured several guest stars including Frankie Avalon, Patrick Macnee, Adrienne Barbeau, Gary Burghoff, Nipsey Russell, Jack Jones, and Jim Hutton.

Jim Hutton was a nice guy, and a few months after he appeared on our show, he died unexpectedly, on June 2, 1979. He drank himself to death. Sadly, he didn't live to see his son, Timothy, win an Oscar just two years later for his outstanding performance in *Ordinary People.*

The show's format was: each week a different group of twelve finalists were in the running for a one-million-dollar tax-free, top prize in a state lottery. Each episode concentrated on the lives of three finalists as the drawing approached.

I felt the anthology of stories worked well in the two-hour pilot, but not on a weekly series. I asked one of the show's executives to go to lunch with me so that I could tell him how to improve the series, but he kept putting me off. In exasperation, I told him, "Look, why don't you whittle the stories down to two stories a week? You can't lock the audience into the plot with so many characters to follow." The executive looked right through me and didn't say a word. *$weepstake$* was canceled after eleven episodes. The show obviously didn't hit the jackpot with television viewers.

* * * * *

My consumption level at the time was not only growing, but I was graduating to much stronger levels of alcohol. I remember a friend giving me a case of vodka. I stored it in the back of my car to always have it nearby. Two weeks later, I checked the trunk, and the whole case was gone.

Then there was the time David Janssen was hosting a tennis tournament at the Riviera Hotel in Las Vegas. I was asked to play along with Kirk Douglas, and the three of us were having our drinks in the LAX airport VIP lounge. David and Kirk started to head for the plane but I wanted one more for the road knowing full well I could have had liquor on board the plane.

I had carry-on luggage only, so having knocked back my drink, I went directly to the plane, spotted a seat next to the window, and sat down. I looked around and didn't see David or Kirk and thought, *Gee, this is weird.* I then opened up a book and started to read, and all of a sudden, we're up, up, and away. I looked out of the window. The plane was heading north. I thought, *Well, somehow they'll turn it back in the right direction.*

After forty-five minutes I still wasn't getting it, but I knew something was wrong. I leaned over to the man sitting next to me and asked, "This plane is going to Las Vegas, isn't it?" He looked at me like I was out of my mind. "Try Salt Lake City."

Salt Lake City was a two-and-a-half-hour flight from Los Angeles, and I thought that once I got there, I'd just buy a ticket straight to Las Vegas. No dice. Back then, as it is today, Salt Lake City is the

Mormon capital of the world, and they didn't have direct flights from Salt Lake City to Sin City. I'd have to fly back to Los Angeles and take another plane to Vegas. In addition, the airport had no place for me to buy a drink. I started to hear the theme from the *Twilight Zone.*

I arrived in Las Vegas around ten that night. Everyone had already played tennis, had dinner, and were dancing and drinking. I found David, Kirk, and their wives at a table.

"What happened to you?" Kirk asked.

I relayed my tale of getting on the wrong plane, and they all fell down laughing hysterically that I went through so much hell.

It took me about eight hours to get to Las Vegas when it normally should have taken fifty minutes, all because I needed "one more for the road."

My whole life revolved around liquor. Do I have enough booze? Am I going to run out? If I go out to a restaurant, will they serve it? I would even have Amanda smuggle it in her purse when we went to see a movie. I couldn't go two hours without having a drink.

Alcohol even started to affect my relationship with my son, who meant the world to me. Logan was ashamed to have his friends over, because I'd ramble on and on in a stupor often repeating myself several times. I'd slur my words, and I'm sure they could smell the liquor as well. Kids aren't stupid.

When Logan turned fifteen, he got his learner's permit, and several times he had to drive me around. I'd get so smashed, yet I still had a conscience and was racked with shame, guilt, and remorse. I was a sick person, not an evil or a bad person, but very, very sick. Alcohol was my best friend, and it was a way of life for me. I couldn't be without my beloved liquid, in all of its poisonous glory.

I tried to carefully hide my drinking from Logan, but one way or another, I always got caught. As was my habit, I'd start the morning off with vodka and orange juice. I'd make Logan breakfast then drop him off at school. One morning, he took a sip of my drink, thinking it was plain orange juice.

His face contorted and then he said, "Dad, there's alcohol in this. What is this? It's so early in the morning, why are you drinking *now*?"

I never felt guilt like I had at that moment. My life was going into a tailspin, and I knew I needed help, yet there was nowhere to turn.

My God, what is happening to me? I'd ask myself. *I'm becoming just like my father.*

I don't think I had ever been more hurt than when my son announced one morning, "Dad, I'm going to move back in with Mom."

The pain I had with the pancreatic attacks was nothing compared to the sharp, searing stab I had felt at that moment.

I'd lost my wife, and now, my most cherished son. Alcohol has a funny way of taking away everything you love. But the man upstairs wasn't finished with me yet. I continued to drink. I hadn't hit rock bottom yet. I was definitely on the downward spiral, but some people don't have a bottom, and it was looking like Edd Byrnes was destined for the proverbial bottomless pit. As long as I tipped that bottle into my mouth, I could only count on three certain things: mental institutions, jails, or death.

CHAPTER FIFTEEN

Wheel of Misfortune

QUESTION: Who was the original host of NBC's *Wheel Of Fortune*?

If you answered, "Pat Sajak," you'd be wrong. If you answered, "Chuck Woolery," you'd be wrong. If you answered, "Edd Byrnes," you'd have answered the question correctly.

Yes, it's true. I was the host of the 1980 pilot of *Wheel of Fortune.* Merv Griffin Productions tried unsuccessfully to sell the pilot in 1975 with Chuck Woolery as the host when the show had a different name.

I used to bump into Merv Griffin quite a lot at Musso & Frank Grill in Hollywood and celebrity tennis tournaments. Once he invited me to fly with him in his private airplane to his home in Carmel, California. When I got on the plane with Merv, I had to get bombed. He was a novice pilot, and I didn't like small planes. I asked him cautiously, "Do you know how to fly this?"

He replied, "A little bit."

I spent the weekend playing in a tennis tournament, hosted by Merv. Clint Eastwood participated in this tournament, and he looked so awkward on the court it was embarrassing. He looked good on a horse, but not on the tennis court.

Merv had a exquisite home overlooking the ocean in Pebble Beach. All the rooms in the house were wired with an intercom system. Every morning at seven, all of the guests would be awakened to Merv's voice on the intercom speaker, "Attention. This is your captain. This is your captain. Breakfast is being served downstairs in the dining room in one hour. Please come down in your tennis clothes and gear. Don't be late!"

Merv saw me in my role as a game-show host on *$weepstake$* and thought it would be a great idea if I became a game-show host in real life for his new pilot called *Wheel Of Fortune.* Merv called me, and we spent a couple of hours a day learning the game. He would teach me the lingo, the phrases, and key words.

The money was good, in fact, very good. Merv Griffin Productions would pay me $3,500 a week, which I could get used to real quick. The best part was, if the show sold, and if it was still on the air after three years, my salary would zoom to a million dollars a year, and I'd get a percentage of the show's profits. After all of the years of heartache, bad breaks, and misunderstandings, I had finally hit the jackpot. I was going to be a millionaire.

We rehearsed for two weeks before we shot two half-hour pilots before a live audience. For some reason, I had thought I wasn't drinking during the filming, but was later told by Susan Staffer, the hostess of the show, that I had been sorely mistaken.

"Edd, everyone knew you were drinking wine in your dressing room before and during filming for God's sake," she told me in a tone that left no doubt in my mind that I did a poor job of hiding the fact.

Naturally, I thought no one knew.

The two shows went smoothly, and NBC decided to pick it up. To this day I can still taste the money.

Merv Griffin rented a suite at the Bel Air Hotel for a celebration party. All the NBC brass were there, and, of course, I had good cause to drink that night and got obnoxiously drunk. I was going to be a very rich man.

A few days later, Henry Willson, who was then my agent, called me into his office. He had made the careers of Rock Hudson, Troy Donahue, Tab Hunter, Rory Calhoun, and Lana Turner. Henry was a very dear friend of mine. His trademark was changing almost all of his client's names. For example, Roy Fitzgerald turned into Rock Hudson, and Merle Johnson became Troy Donahue.

"Edd, I've got some good news and some bad news. Which do you want to hear first?"

"The good news."

"Merv Griffin Productions sold the pilot to NBC."

"OK . . . and what about the bad news?"

"I don't know how to tell you this, Edd, but NBC doesn't want you to host the show." He was using his most diplomatic and compassionate tone.

"What the hell are you talking about?" I screamed. "I sold the pilot! They tried selling it once without me, and they didn't succeed. I sold the damned thing, and now they don't want me?"

I wasn't given a reason by the NBC brass, but I knew in the back of my mind that, somehow or another, my drinking may have had a major role.

"Doesn't my contract protect me from this?" I asked Henry.

Ah, that was the key. The contract. Well, my contract was not ironclad. I didn't have it in my contract that if the pilot sold, I came along as the host. I didn't have anything legal to go by, and I was very upset that Henry hadn't protected me. I had no legal grounds to sue. Merv hired Chuck Woolery, who was then replaced by Pat Sajak and Vanna White. The rest is history.

An NBC executive who was at that celebration party told me that I had gotten hostile and arrogant and rubbed a few of the executives the wrong way. They had heard I was drinking during rehearsals and had seen it for themselves, firsthand, just how intoxicated I could become. A friend of mine overheard one NBC executive tell Merv, "We can't have this guy host the show. He'll be drunk every day on the set. Let's get someone who's sober."

I literally drank myself out of a job and millions of dollars. By my estimation, had I remained the host of *Wheel of Fortune* to this day, I might be worth somewhere in the neighborhood of twenty million dollars. As Kirk Douglas's character, Jonathan Shields, said in *The Bad and the Beautiful*, "If you're gonna dream, dream big." And if you're going to lose, lose big.

Later on, I ran into Merv Griffin at the Musso & Frank grill. I held a deep resentment toward him. I told him in a rather unsavory tone of anger, "I worked my ass off for you, Merv, and you didn't hire me."

He never told me, "Edd, it was your drinking." I didn't need to be told that, but I did want to hear it from his own lips why he didn't hire me for *Wheel Of Fortune*. Merv Griffin still hasn't told me to this day, and I hold no grudges toward this man, but just the same, I would like to give him a second chance to make me another offer. (Sure Eddie, sure.)

* * * * *

If I could compare my life at that time to a city, it would have to be Hiroshima: I wasn't just getting bombarded; I was ground zero for the Big One.

My mother had died that year.

Mom was really a sweet lady, a very strong woman, and a very good mother, but I always wanted her to be like Myrna Loy or Greer Garson, an elegant, refined lady. She was never like that. She had to work in sweatshops to feed her children, and she had no time to dress up like June Allyson. She never sported a dress, pearls, and an Eisenhower apron. It was only later that I came to accept her for what she was: a survivor, in the truest sense of the word.

There were a few issues that separated us from becoming closer emotionally. Chief among them was she didn't respect men. She told me once, before passing on, "Men are only to be used."

I could never be sober around her. My mother pushed all my buttons and then some. I know she was very proud of me and the success I had achieved, but she was very tough to be with. She'd put me down in subtle, "little" ways that doubly hurt my feelings. For instance, I'd want to take her to dinner, and she'd say, "I don't want you to spend your money on me. It's much too expensive." The way she said this implied I couldn't afford it. My mother wouldn't give me the pleasure of taking her out for dinner or spoiling her with gifts, all of which were intended to show that I owed her a debt of gratitude. I simply wanted to pay her back for the years of scraping by.

If I had to guess, I would assume she never worked out her relationship with her own father, and she certainly ran into the Department of Bad Luck with my father.

My mother was suffering from Lou Gehrig's disease, which is progressive and fatal. In my alcoholic state, it was hard for me to deal with this situation. It got to the point where she couldn't open the car door, and then later when it got much worse, she couldn't even remember my name.

My sister, Jo-Ann, had been living with my mother for a number of years. She called me one night and said in a somber tone, "Mom's in bad shape."

"Where are you going to be?" I asked.

She told me she would take mother to Brotman Memorial Hospital in Culver City. The one and the same hospital where movie star Jeff Chandler died during a simple operation. It had a horrible reputation, and this was where my mother was going to stay? I caught up with them in the lobby. We put Mom into a wheelchair, rode the elevator to her floor, and wheeled her to her bed.

I kissed her on the forehead and said, "I'll come around in the morning to see you." She nodded as though she understood me, and I walked out the door.

Around five that morning, my sister called to tell me, "Mom's dying." But there was more. "The doctors want to know if we should allow for a tracheotomy to let her breathe?"

"What exactly does that mean?" I asked.

"It means she might only live for another twenty-four hours."

I didn't know what to say. "Well, what do you think?" I asked my sister. "You are much closer to her than I am." I was leaving her with the difficult task of making a life-or-death decision.

"I don't think Mom would like it," she said, leaving in my mind no question that women are the stronger of the two sexes.

About an hour later, my mother passed away.

Funeral arrangements were made to ship her body back to New York to be beside her husband, my father. I had never seen his gravesite, and Jo-Ann made all of the arrangements. All I had to do was show up, which I didn't.

Like the good alcoholic that I was, I couldn't deal with the situation and went off to Puerto Vallarta with Amanda, in an attempt to escape reality. I went on a ten-day vacation/drinking binge and left Jo-Ann to attend to everything herself. I wasn't supportive at all. While I'd taken the blasting of Hiroshima, I had yet to hear of Nagasaki.

* * * * *

For years, Connie Stevens has hosted a Christmas party at her home in Holmby Hills. There would be a tent, band, and assorted buffets of delicacies. Her ex-husbands were always invited, which made it all the more interesting. It's a first-class event.

That Christmas of 1980, I attended her party alone and got plastered. I drank throughout the entire evening and thought, *There's no way I can get home tonight.* I thought I would go up to one of her rooms and sleep for the night, wake up in the morning, and then drive home. Then I had another thought, *Nah, I'll just go outside, take a couple of deep breaths of fresh air, sober up, and then drive home.*

To this day, I have no idea how I got home. It was quite a drive from Connie's house to my place in Los Angeles. I had to negotiate down winding roads to reach Sunset Boulevard and then through Beverly Hills to reach my destination.

I woke up the next morning, or, rather came to, around ten with all of my clothes on. I went to the front door, and it was standing wide open. When I went to close it, I spotted my car parked on the front lawn. It scared the hell out of me. I don't remember a thing about that night or how I got home, but it was definitely a wake-up call. Somebody could have come in and robbed me, or worse, killed me like my good friend Jay Sebring in the Manson slayings off Benedict Canyon.

I knew Jay when he was Jay Kummer. He had this little apartment and roomed with another guy named Richard Curtis. Jay's hobby at the time was cutting hair, and he did mine for fifty cents.

Jay didn't have his shop then. He mainly hung out and smoked grass. If you had told me that he would later become one of the premiere hairstylists in Beverly Hills, I would have laughed in your face.

Later on he changed his name to Jay Sebring, and it was R. J. Wagner who told me about this great hairstylist on Rodeo Drive.

Jay had found fame and fortune and lived in a mansion that used to belong to Jean Harlow. Jay was one of the people murdered by Charles Manson's hippie cult. He died in a very gruesome manner, all because they left the front door unlocked. I not only left the front door to my house unlocked, but left it wide open, all because of my drinking.

My erratic behavior continued when, in November of 1981, I called my "cousin," Dr. Francis Wolfort, who was a widely known and highly respected plastic surgeon in Boston. I was getting some bags under my eyes from the late nights and the boozing, so Frank fit me into his tight schedule. Frank, Joe Finn, and I had been friends in New York when Frank was attending medical school.

I bought two round-trip tickets from Los Angeles to Boston for Amanda and me, and we spent the night at Frank and his wife, Florene's house in Wellesley Hills. That next morning at 6:30, I was scheduled for the operation.

As we were driving to the hospital, I got the jitters. When I was getting prepped for surgery, I became really nervous and said to Amanda, "I don't know if I can go through with this." She replied, "Edd, c'mon, we've flown all the way from Los Angeles to get this done, so it's final."

Frank stepped into the room donning his green medical scrubs and ready to go. "Frank, I don't think I can go through with this," I pleaded. He pulled out his stethoscope, put it to my heart, and said, "Your heart is racing pretty fast. Well, whatever you want to do, but we do have everyone ready to go in the operating room." The ball was in my court.

"I just don't think I can go through with this right now," and I got up, got dressed, hailed a taxi, and headed for the Ritz Hotel for a morning cocktail.

Six months later, I called Frank again, having decided the bags under my eyes were really getting bad. "Frank, I want the operation now," I said in a playful tone, but he knew I was serious.

"You're not going to change your mind again, are you, Edd?" he replied, just as playful.

I assured him I was going to go through with the operation. Frank went through the same procedure as last time. He booked the operating room, got his people ready, and Amanda and I flew to Boston. I went through with it this time.

When I was wheeled out of the operating room, Amanda came up to me to see how I was recuperating. My eyes were all black and blue, and there was still some blood around them. Amanda took one look at me and passed out on the spot. Fainted dead away. She had to be revived with smelling salts, and they placed her in the recovery room bed right next to me. It was all a part of this crazy alcoholic life of mine.

On the morning of November 29, 1981, I was getting ready to play tennis with a friend. It was pretty early for me, and I had yet to shake off the cobwebs, when my friend asked me, "Did you hear about Natalie?"

"Natalie who?" I asked, not all there.

"Natalie Wood."

Instantly I got a sinking feeling in my stomach. "No," I cautiously replied.

"Well," he paused, "she drowned off the coast of Catalina. Natalie, R. J., and Christopher Walken were all spending the weekend on their yacht, *Splendour*."

I was dealt a major blow to my system. Natalie was so young, so full of vitality, and I could not imagine her drowning of all things. I used to see her swim in her pool all the time.

It's one of life's bitter ironies that this talented young woman, who was an actress her whole life, and gave us so many wonderful performances, is remembered more for her dramatic death than for her achievements on the silver screen.

I think of Natalie often today, her beautiful smile, the warmth she radiated, and how everyone loved her so much. She was one in a million and always very generous with her friends and relatives.

Like a rose, Natalie Wood died young and beautiful.

* * * * *

Surprisingly, Amanda never left me because of my drinking. She was twenty-four, and she had been by my side for five years. She had been wanting to get married, and she stuck it out for as long as she could. It was the same exact point that I had brought Asa to, "Either we get married or I have to leave."

"You don't want to marry me," I warned.

Deep down I had a streak of insecurity, no less than a mile wide. I felt I would ruin this gentle soul's life if she married me.

"Well, you told me one day you'd kick me out, and I guess I'm fleeing the nest." Amanda's words pierced my heart. I knew at that moment that our relationship was over.

The pain wasn't as deep as when Asa left, but it ran a very close second. These were probably the two loves of my life, Asa and Amanda, and I drove them both away because I couldn't make a commitment to either one.

When Amanda left, I went into a serious depression. I didn't realize how much I loved her until after she left. I sank into a deep, dark hole, and my personality radically changed. Oh, how I changed.

Seeking some sort of refuge, I flew to El Paso for a tennis tournament. Actor Doug McClure and I were knocking 'em down pretty good in the hotel bar. When I got back to my room, I was feeling very lonely and pretty despondent over the loss of Amanda. I mustered up the nerve to call her and pleaded with her to take me back.

"Edd, we can't get back together. It's over," her bittersweet words rang in my ears.

My room was five stories up from the ground. As I looked down over the pavement, I had an anxiety attack and thought of throwing myself out the window to take away the misery I was feeling at the moment.

I had drowned myself with wine throughout the day but found no relief from the churning in my stomach that only a lost love can cause.

I called the front desk and said, "Would you please call a doctor and get him up here as fast as you can. I'm hurting and in agony."

A couple of minutes later, two men in dark suits appeared at my door, each holding what looked like a Bible. After a few minutes of them talking about my drinking problem, I hastily asked them, "Where's your medical bag? You've gotta give me a fix. Anything to calm me down. Give me some pills!" I demanded in desperation.

My demands were met with stony silence. I reacted by kicking them out of my room. I had no idea who they were, but they couldn't produce, so I went down to the hotel bar again and threw back a couple of shots of vodka to numb myself. Since the wine wasn't working, the vodka certainly would. In no time, I passed out in my room to that comfortable place I then called Nirvana. It was lights out.

Alcohol is a depressant, and it eventually altered my perception and thinking. When Amanda left, I drank myself into oblivion. I became so paranoid, I thought somebody out there was coming to get me.

There would be periods where I would get paranoid, and then it would go away. Sometimes I'd stay in the house for three days straight, never seeing the light of day. In brief moments of sanity, I'd ask myself, *How am I going to get myself out of this situation? How can I get my life back in order?* But when I was drinking, I couldn't get my life back in order. There's no way. No way in hell, which is what my life was gradually becoming.

I could stay sober, but not alone. I would go on the wagon, but as soon as a television show or movie was over, I would fall off again.

The alcoholic has a tendency to isolate himself from society, and that's exactly what I was doing.

I felt like a fugitive on the run, and I had to protect myself at whatever the cost.

I took out my hammer and nailed all of the windows shut, closed the shutters, and turned out the lights. In the end, I would watch television on my sofa with a shotgun sitting across my lap, just in case "they" were trying to get me. Who exactly "they" were, I didn't know, but I was ready for them when they came through my front door.

Everytime I heard a noise, I'd go over to the shutters and peek out, my scattergun cocked and loaded.

And yet, I still hadn't hit rock bottom. I was determined to keep drinking at any cost. That included losing my sanity, which was slowly giving way.

CHAPTER SIXTEEN

My Name Is Edd B.

IT WAS MY son, Logan, who finally said something to shake my foundation, but not directly to me. He told Asa, "Dad's beginning to worry me. He's drinking too much."

How ironic it was that my ex-wife Asa would bring me to my first 12-step meeting. I wouldn't have gone with anyone else because my ego and pride were disproportionate to reality. I was once told that ego meant, "E-G-O . . . Edging God Out." How true. How true.

"Edd, do it for Logan. Do it for yourself!" Asa pleaded, and so I went.

I had been drinking all day, and when I attended that first meeting, I came with a wineglass in my hand. It was nothing unusual to me because at that time, I had been carrying my wine with me wherever I went. Even today, I'm still amazed at my irreverence and lack of respect.

At that first meeting was a famous actor, who was sober for the moment, and he kept repeating, "I wish I had some tequila right about now." He was mumbling and moaning, and right away I was judging him. *What a pathetic loser!* I thought.

In addition, the room was filled with smoke. One addiction usually replaces another, and a lot of alcoholics turn in the bottle for cigarettes.

Asa felt that I would somehow "connect" with this actor, but there was no connection at the time. I left that meeting and continued to drink for another six months to a year. It was all a blur.

My consumption level at this point reached an all-time high. I'd start the morning off with three glasses of vodka and fresh orange juice (I thought I'd drink *something* healthy) and then I'd try to eat breakfast. I'd drink around three or four bottles of wine during the course of the day before calling it quits around 8:30 P.M.

Logan would say, "Dad, it's so early, and you're going to bed already?" By then, I wasn't "going to bed" but merely "passing out."

I am ending up just like my father, I said to myself before the oblivion came to greet me. *I am a drunk, I am a failure.*

Eventually, with yet another trying effort, Asa came to my rescue. I had been drinking all day, but she persuaded me to attend a seven o'clock meeting in Brentwood on a Thursday night.

With wineglass in hand, I spotted another movie star there, and it shocked me when he came up and greeted me warmly. This was none other than my old rival and only threat to the teen idol throne at Warner Brothers, my formidable foe, Mr. Troy Donahue.

Troy looked at me and said, "You look pretty bad. Maybe you should check into a hospital."

I shrugged off his comment. Several other people came over, people with years of sobriety, and they hugged me. One after another, they hugged me. This was something I hadn't experienced in a very long time. They understood me. They understood what I was going through, what my emotions were and what I was thinking. It was the last gas station before I crossed the desert and surrendered.

A veritable caravan of people escorted me to St. John's Hospital for a thirty-day dry-out session. A doctor at that meeting pulled a few strings and managed to get me into St. John's with a private room that night. I began to get scared. Perhaps "freaking out" might have been more appropriate, for I had to be given Valium. My support group then took over and started caring for me, with Troy as the leader of this pack.

"Stay here tonight, Edd. We'll be back tomorrow to see you. Just don't drink for tonight," was his message. "Try to get some sleep."

Finally, I was left all alone, and there was no love surrounding me any longer. This hospital lacked the two things I desperately wanted at the time, a good twenty-seven-inch color television and a chilled bottle of Wente Brothers Chablis. These were conveniently waiting for me at my house.

I felt I needed a drink desperately, so I got out of my bed, got dressed, and at 2:00 A.M. , began walking down the hospital corridor toward the nearest exit sign.

"Mr. Byrnes, where are you going?" asked an orderly behind me.

I still had the keys to my car in my pants pocket and made a mad dash for the car. By the grace of God, I made it home safely and opened the refrigerator. There were my best friends, or so I thought at the time, Charles Krug and Wente Brothers Chablis. I poured myself a nice, cool, very tall glass of wine and chased it down with a sleeping pill. I slept the sleep of the dead until Troy Donahue woke me up with an early morning phone call.

"I heard you escaped from the hospital," he said.

Boy, news travels fast around these here parts. I confirmed the news.

"Have you had a drink today?" Troy asked me.

"Not yet."

"GOOD. DON'T DRINK!"

For some reason, I asked, "Why not?"

He got adamant. "CAN YOU JUST NOT DRINK NOW? *PLEASE*!"

Boy, these recovering alcoholics sure can get testy.

"All right. I won't drink," I promised.

Troy then asked, "Can you drive?"

"Yes," I said.

"Good. Can you meet me at Eighteenth Street and California at 10:45 this morning?"

For some strange reason, I kept my word to Troy and didn't have a drink.

Right on schedule, we got together and went to this meeting in a church basement. At every 12-step meeting, they ask, "Are there any alcoholics in this room?" Everyone in the meeting raised their hands, that is, everyone except for the scared Eddie Breitenberger. I just sat there, not raising my hand because I didn't think I was an alcoholic.

Boy, was I smart. The next question was, "Are there any *newcomer* alcoholics in this room?" That was my cue, and I hadn't missed a cue in twenty-five years.

Troy leaned over and whispered, "Edd, raise your hand," and with a little help from my friend, my hand went up in the air.

I finally had the strength to stand on my own two feet, and the moment of truth had come. I had been running down this road for twelve years, and I was out of pavement. I was staring straight into the abyss, and the demons of my past were snapping at my heels.

Do I stay or do I go?

Do I sink or do I swim?

DO I LIVE OR DO I DIE?

Those questions swirled furiously around inside my head as I contemplated the most important decision of my life.

It was as if some alien being had invaded my body when I managed to say, "[sniff] my name is . . . [more sniffles] Edd, and I'm . . . an . . . I'm an alcoholic. . . . " I began to weep like a child. People in the crowd started applauding. It was incredible. I had never gotten applause like that on stage, and I wasn't even acting!

It was as if this huge weight was lifted off my shoulders, and it was probably as close to a spiritual experience as I've ever had. I *never* thought of myself as an alcoholic. I was driving in an expensive car, going to posh restaurants, tasting fine wines, and living the good life. I thought alcoholics were just a bunch of bums who lived on park benches, drinking out of brown paper bags.

At first, that was my attitude toward the whole meeting. I expected people in old clothes, all losers, smoking cigarettes, sitting around telling boring war stories. Yet, when I got there, everybody was nice, well-dressed, successful people, laughing, talking, eating doughnuts and drinking coffee, all the while saying, "Welcome, Edd. It's really nice to see you." I was in a total daze.

At this point, I finally admitted and accepted that I was an alcoholic. A friend at that meeting told me something that I will never forget: "Alcoholics are not bad people, just sick people who are trying to get well." At midday, on the date of August 6, 1982, I was finally experiencing an entirely different experience: it was my first day of sobriety in many, many years.

* * * * *

If you think I was instantly healed, you're dead wrong. As a matter of fact, Troy and I went to lunch right after that meeting, and I had the audacity to order a drink in front of him.

"No, don't drink today," Troy urged. "Just don't drink today." He then asked, "Where do you live?"

I told him. He asked if I lived alone. "Yes, my son, Logan, just moved out and I'm living on my own."

"Good. We'll swing by my house first, I'll pack some clothes, and I'm going to move in with you for a couple of days." Troy didn't merely suggest this, his tone made it a statement of fact.

"What for?" I asked suspiciously.

"You're going to keep me sober," Troy said.

"I'm going to keep you sober?" I asked, with my entire face conveying a look of surprise. "I see."

Troy packed his clothes, moved in with me, and basically babysat me for four days. All the while, he took me to meetings. We attended morning meetings, afternoon meetings, and evening meetings. THREE TIMES A DAY! I went to so many meetings that I began to resent it. If I attended one more meeting, I was going to reach for a bottle.

That Sunday afternoon, after three days of bodyguarding me, I told Troy I was going to get the Sunday paper.

"You're not going to go out and get a drink, are you, Edd?" said my watchkeeper.

"No, just a paper," I said innocently.

"Are you sure?" asked the inquiring mind.

I went out, got the paper, and came right back. I wanted Troy to trust me, and I kept my word. I didn't have a drink, but God how I wanted to.

Now it was Monday, and I had four days of sobriety under my belt. That night we attended another meeting together, and at the end of it, Troy said, "I'm cutting you loose. You haven't had a drink in nearly four days. Just don't drink tonight. And in the morning, ask your higher power for the strength to stay sober and get to a meeting."

After that fourth day of sobriety, I started to change my thinking pattern. I was willing not to drink for five minutes at a time, then I graduated to ten minutes at a time, and I took it from there, though this was not my intention in the beginning.

All throughout this time, I spent countless hours on the phone with other members, talking and crying until early in the morning when I was so tired that I just fell asleep. I was frantic without a drink.

I'd cry, "I can't sleep! I can't sleep! I'm up and I don't know what to do."

I also quit taking the sleeping pills. I was kicking two bad habits at once. One of my mentors told me, "Nobody ever died from a lack of sleep, Edd." It would take years for my body to return to its natural state from the alcohol and sleeping pills, but now I was dearly paying for it with fits of insomnia.

I thought that I might not be able to resist having a drink for thirty days and get my life together. I believed that when I "got it together," I could start drinking all over again, but this time drink like a gentleman and not let myself get out of control as I did before.

The more meetings I attended and the more I talked to my fellow alcoholics, the more I learned about the disease of alcoholism. That it is truly a disease, and it is progressive, terminal, and an obsession of the mind, coupled with an allergy of the body. I knew in my heart of hearts that I could not drink like a gentleman again and that I was powerless over alcohol and it made my life unmanageable.

As I racked up more and more days of sobriety, I became stronger and stronger. The obsession to drink left me after my first ninety days of sobriety and many sleepless nights crying into the telephone. With some people, that desire never leaves, so I could count this single blessing as a miracle. That didn't mean I didn't have temptations every now and then. I learned something new every day.

I had to do anything it took not to take a drink. In fact, I was too afraid to drink once I realized that I might die if I drank again. I was willing to take direction. I was willing to go three times a day to meetings if that's what it took.

About six months into my sobriety, the temptation to drink almost got the best of me. Asa and I were checking out some colleges for Logan, and the three of us flew into Denver and rented a car to drive to Boulder.

Asa was driving while I did the navigating. We somehow got lost on the freeway and my dear ex-wife abruptly stopped the car in the middle lane while traffic was flowing rather nicely.

"You drive!" she screamed.

I started to freak out because she didn't even pull over to the side of the road. We were almost rear-ended, and horns were blowing all over the freeway. Asa would not move the car, she just sat there, staring at me. I screamed at her, and Logan began to cry in the backseat. It was a nightmare.

I got out of the car, opened the trunk, grabbed my luggage, slammed the trunk shut, and ran across the freeway to a hotel at the next exit.

I somehow made it to the hotel, and I knew there would be a lobby with a bar in it. Boy, did I need a drink *real bad.* The first thing I spotted was the bar. It was about as inviting as a drink of water to a man who had just crawled across the Sahara Desert. The music was playing, people were laughing. It was the cocktail hour. It was time to make a decision.

Do I get a drink, or do I pick up a phone and call my sponsor?

I went straight to the pay phone in the lobby and dialed the numbers of my sponsor, who could offer me wisdom and calm me down. He wasn't in, and I dialed the number of another fellow alcoholic, but he wasn't in either. I dialed two more alcoholics and in each case, got no answer. I was definitely biting the bullet. I was also in town for a tennis tournament and arranged it so that someone could pick me up and take me to Vail. I hadn't thought of God in years, ever since I was an altar boy in New York. My higher power had always been alcohol, but with the saying of the serenity prayer, over and over, "God, grant me the serenity to accept the things I cannot change, the courage to change the things I can and the wisdom to know the difference." I made it through that day without taking a drink, and I made a new friend in the process. God.

What I later discovered was never to put myself in a stressful situation that might cause me to drink. I learned never to get in a car with Asa again, a promise I have kept to this day. It was one "slippery spot" that I could ill afford.

I was told early in my sobriety, "Edd, if you're ever in an uncomfortable situation and those old feelings start to come up to where you might want to drink, get out of that situation immediately. Just get up and leave and don't apologize. Just get out of there."

After the first year of sobriety, I felt as if I was no longer a visitor at the meetings. I felt as if I belonged. I didn't have to pretend any longer, but there were still things that I didn't fully understand. I was told, "Edd, suit up and show up and get there on time." To this day, I'm never late for anything. If I am late, I am debting because I am not getting the most for myself.

Three years into my sobriety, I was rehearsing a Clifford Odets play called *The Big Knife* in London, when a Scottish director became very abusive towards me. I had accepted the play and had to hurry to England to open the play in six weeks. I read it for the first time on the plane, and the next day I had a read-through with the cast.

The cast had the luxury of having the script for six weeks already. The director had ordered them to know their lines and have them completely memorized before the first day of rehearsal. I, on the other hand, had only read the play once, while they had the six weeks to prepare. However, with all that time before the opening, I felt there was plenty of time for me to learn the lines. After the fifth day of rehearsal, the director came up to me and said, "Edd, I don't think you can do this."

I thought he was kidding. "What do you mean?" I chuckled.

"I don't think you're ready. I don't think you can handle this," said my little Scottish friend.

Again, thinking he was carrying the joke to the *nth* degree, I smiled and said, "You must be joking."

"No, Edd. I'm not joking. I don't think you can do this. You don't know all of your lines yet."

The man left me speechless. It was like an adult chastising this little kid, and I couldn't for the life of me speak. I got all choked up. It was like I was that twelve-year-old boy in school when the nuns told me, "You're dumb, Eddie. You're stupid." All of a sudden, Eddie Breitenberger was reacting to this director, and my voice went silent.

I managed to whisper, "I'm going home now. I'll call you later." I left the stage and went back to the Sloane Club where I was staying. I called my good friend and fellow actor, Anthony Hopkins, and asked him to have a cup of coffee with me.

Tony is a recovering alcoholic, and I'm not breaking his anonymity because he has discussed his drinking days in television interviews many times. He is, of course, one of the best actors in the world. I hadn't signed a contract as of yet, and I told Tony over the phone of my predicament. Tony said, "Of course I'll meet with you."

Tony then told me a story of when director John Dexter became very abusive towards him in a play. To my surprise, the Academy Award–winning actor told him, "I quit."

"Edd," he suggested, "Your sobriety is the number one priority in your life now. If this situation is upsetting you, then I suggest you get out of it. You don't want those feelings coming up and the temptation to drink." He also told me that I was in a foreign country and was away from my strong support group of men.

Tony's words soothed me and helped me to become strong again. I went the next morning to see the producer, Bill Kenwright, and told him, "I won't hurry up and memorize my lines. We've got five weeks left to rehearse. Why don't you just give me two days off, and I'll stay at the motel and memorize the whole damned play?"

Bill gave in to my demands, but when I got back to the club, he called and said the director, that ballsy little weasel, wanted me to come to his office and perform one of the scenes. I hadn't auditioned in twenty-five years, and now this little shit was really testing my patience.

Again, I went to Bill's office to thank him for offering me the part and to say good-bye.

"What can we do to keep you on? Do you want the director fired? I'll do it if that's what it takes to keep you."

"No," I replied, "I'm out of here." But not before he insisted he show me his new prized possession, the suede shirt that Alan Ladd had worn in the movie *Shane*, which Bill Kenwright had just bought in an auction.

I left that next day, deeply hurt and disappointed in myself. To take revenge upon that director and have him fired would have felt good for the time being, but I later learned that resentments will help the alcoholic to run to the nearest bar. Instead, I took the high road and extricated myself from a very bad situation. A friend told me that *The Big Knife* closed after two weeks and was considered a major flop. Maybe the man upstairs was just looking out for me.

It was the first time that a situation like this had ever happened to me, but that was a major turning point: my sobriety had become the number one priority in my life.

CHAPTER SEVENTEEN

Solvency & Prosperity

HAVE YOU HEARD the axiom "One addiction replaces another addiction"? I didn't replace my craving for alcohol with a substitute, such as eating, smoking, sex, or some other type of "binge." No indeed. My replacement for giving up the booze was spending money. I was replacing the alcohol with another fix, and I nearly fixed myself into a hole.

From 1982 to 1985, I did some serious spending and went into debt. I was no longer earning the high amount of money that I once did. However, I was spending more than was coming in. Those days of three thousand dollars a week were long gone, but I was still living like I was earning at least that much. This is commonly called "getting into the red."

I began to max out all my credit cards, and my life was spinning out of control again. Nothing will make an alcoholic go back to the bottle faster than financial problems.

John Harjes used to ask me, "Now Eddie, are you saving something for a rainy day?" The answer, quite truthfully, was a simple and honest "no." For almost a decade I had no real savings account. I just lived for the day with no thought for tomorrow. I had never thought about a financial life, because there was no one to teach me. I was only taught how to earn money, how to spend it, but not save it.

One day while I was in a 12-step meeting, I was telling a friend about my financial woes. "No matter how much money I'm earning, it never seems to be enough. I'm in debt and it just seems as if I don't know how to get out. There's no solution."

My friend had a suggestion. "There's another 12-step program that addresses debt. Maybe you'd better check it out." He was very frank in telling me, "It's all about getting your financial affairs in order. It's about living abundantly, taking charge of your life, and not debting, no matter what, one day at a time."

"Romance and finance" problems are common among alcoholics.

After several sleepless nights, with my palms sweaty, I knew I needed to get out of debt and get solvent.

I hit my financial bottom in 1985, and miraculously, I didn't drink over my new crisis. Just like I did for the alcohol, I had to go and get help for my financial life.

I learned from that program that, just like drinking, I don't debt one day at a time. At present, I don't drink one day at a time, and I don't debt one day at a time.

I also had to carry a notepad with me and write down everything that I spent for that day. I objected to that one.

"C'mon, you mean to tell me that if I go out and spend fifty cents on a lousy newspaper, I have to write it down on this pad of paper?"

"Yes," I was told.

I had a bad attitude and didn't want to do this right away. I kicked and screamed, but I became willing to take that first step.

That first step was to be able to admit that I was powerless over compulsive debting and my life had become unmanageable. Sound familiar?

Then I was told to cut up my beloved credit cards and make up a new repayment plan. Oh, how that hurt! It was like taking the scissors to my child. I had always used the cards for everything, and because of my jet-set lifestyle, my fingertips rarely touched currency.

Money is spiritual and has energy, by its very nature. It so boldly states on all currency, "In God We Trust." I slowly began to learn that instead of filling my car with gas and handing the cashier my credit card, I would hand him a twenty-dollar bill or, if I didn't have a twenty-dollar bill, I'd hand him a five. Whatever I could in order not to debt one day at a time. I eventually discovered that I wouldn't receive a bill at the end of the month if I kept repeating this process. God, what a concept! Would this mean that I would never get another bill from another gas station if I kept doing this? My God, what a concept!

Eventually it became habit forming, my writing down all my expenses. "Lunch—$7.00; Dry Cleaning—$18.00; Car Wash—$8.75; Photos—$40.00; Parking—$2.75; Movie—$7.00," and so on. I'd continually write it down, enter the numbers into a big book, and add it all up. For six weeks, I practiced this ritual faithfully and wrote down on the other side of the ledger how much money was coming in. In no time at all, I discovered that I did have money in my life.

After six weeks of keeping track of my money, I asked to have a "pressure meeting" to take all the pressure off me, to put Edd "number one" and my creditors at the bottom of the list. I wrote a letter to all those to whom I owed and told them that they weren't going to be paid back as fast as they'd like, but I would show them a willingness to repay them.

I had a list of ten creditors. I wrote that I was going on a moratorium for three months and that they would be paid back in full. It might not be as fast as they would like, but they would get all their money. I could take vacations, I could go to the movies, I could take a friend to lunch, and then I could pay back my creditors.

When I went on moratorium, I was taking charge of my life again. I wrote, "You are going to get your money, this is how you're going to get your money, but I am in charge. You are not in charge." That's the fear that everybody has of their creditors. They think that their creditors are in charge. They think that their creditors are mommy or daddy.

The list of my personal debts to my friends were paid off first, because they meant more to me. I then paid off all my business creditors and became solvent again after a few years. As long as I'm not incurring any new debts, I'm in recovery.

When I hit my financial bottom, I pawned a Cartier wristwatch that Asa had bought for me when Logan was born. It was such a beautiful watch that when Bill Holden and I were on a plane together, he had noticed it and commented, "That watch will last you a hundred years."

In 1985 I had to pawn the watch for $500 because I needed some fast money. The watch was worth in the neighborhood of $5,000. A few days later, I was so upset about the watch that I broke down and cried in front of two of my friends from the program.

"Edd, this watch is really affecting you. The first thing you have to do is get that watch back," I was told by my friends. The sentimental value was so powerful that I returned to the pawnshop and got it out of hock. I was charged interest to get it back, but it was worth it. I still have it today.

I learned from the program that pawning your possessions is equivalent to getting a temporary fix. It's a shot of heroin. It's a shot of vodka. It's like getting open-heart surgery and putting a Band-Aid over the wound. All it does is stop the bleeding for a few minutes. It's a temporary solution to a major problem.

Gradually I was getting my life together. I began putting my money into a savings account, but most importantly, I was no longer living beyond my means. Today, I do what I want to do and have a good life, and I'm still very active in the program.

I no longer live in a fantasy world, but in reality. I don't borrow anything from anybody, but I also don't lend. If anyone asks me, "Edd, can I borrow twenty dollars?" I'll say, "No, I won't lend it to you, but I'll give it to you as a gift." This is so I won't build up resentment toward that person. Resentments lead to drinking, and drinking to spending.

Back when I was living high on the hog, it would have been nothing for me, on a whim and the spur of the moment, to take a woman to Europe. Remember romance and finance? Today, if a woman that I cared about wanted me to take her to Europe, I could take her there, or I could say, "I'd love to take you to Europe, but right now it's not in my spending plan." I don't say, "I can't afford it," rather I reply in a more positive way.

I remember I took a trip with Logan to Hawaii in 1979 right after *$weepstake$* was canceled. We flew first class from Hawaii to Italy, then took a cruise ship from Genoa, down the coast to Portofino. From there, we took a train to Sperlonga and visited Raf Vallone. The vacation cost me around ten thousand dollars, but that's what I *used* to do when I got depressed. I am no longer so foolish with my money.

As I stated before, I never really had anyone to teach me about money. When I first came to California, I took money from my friend Joe Finn and borrowed money from an acting teacher named Val Dufour, who would lend it to me at 10 percent interest. I started borrowing at an early age.

The most important thing about debt that I have to continuously remind myself is, that *I am not my debt. I am not my car, and I am not my job. I am not how much or how little money I have in the bank.* Steve Trilling, an executive at Warner Brothers under J. L. Warner, committed suicide after he was fired. He must have thought he was his job. When his job no longer existed, he killed himself. I've actually known quite a few people like that. When they're out of a job, they either drink themselves to death or commit suicide. What a shame to think that being fired from a job is a potential life or death situation.

The greatest gift that I can give myself today is to not spend more money than I earn.

* * * * *

It was wreckage of the past that I wanted to make amends for. That included those loved ones I had hurt by my drinking and all those relationships I had almost ruined.

I remember a few years back running into a director in London for whom I once worked on a British television program called *A Yank in the RAF.* This was during my years of hard drinking in the early seventies. I asked him, "Was I drinking pretty heavily back then?" Being the proper English gentleman that he was, he said, "Edd, we were all drinking heavily in those days." In any event, I apologized to him for my past behavior.

I hadn't seen Amanda for quite some time. I was driving on La Cienega Boulevard when I spotted those long, magnificent legs. I knew in an instant it was she. I got out of the car and followed her into the art gallery that she had entered.

I was the only person who ever called her Mandy, so I went inside without delay and said, "Hello, Mandy." She knew it was me right away.

She was very excited to see me since we hadn't seen each other in a year. We embraced in a long hug. The next night was New Year's Eve, and I asked her to bring in the New Year with me. Now that I was sober, I thought we might be able to make a fresh start. I was hoping that we'd find romance once again.

We went to our favorite restaurant, Musso & Frank, in the company of my sponsor, Dan B., and his wife, Rose. They invited us back to their condominium after dinner for coffee, but we politely declined and said we were going home to make love. My recovery involves honesty to myself and others, and so I told Dan like it was. "Dan, really, we don't want to go back to your condo for coffee. Amanda and I are going home to make love." He and Rose laughed at my candor and wished us well.

When Amanda and I got to my place, we followed through with our plans. It was great experience and yet, it was very different—I was sober. It was almost like trying to revive something that just wasn't there. Amanda ended up spending the night, but left the next morning.

I invited her over for dinner that evening, and she said that would be very nice. She called me a little bit later that day and said she couldn't make it.

I was very disappointed.

"No really, I can't come over tonight," she responded, sounding a bit uncomfortable.

Amanda never called back, and I never called her again. I knew it was over for good. I accepted that, and I didn't have to drink because of it.

I think in hindsight that she didn't want to go through the pain again. When one person stops drinking, although Amanda was never an alcoholic, the relationship changes.

I last heard about Amanda through a mutual friend. She had finally married, which is what she always wanted. For her sake, I hope she's happy and healthy. I only wish her the very best, for she deserves it. And Mandy, get your first serve in this time around!

I took a while, but I made my way to Asa and apologized to her for all of the heartache I had put her through, AND GOD BLESS THAT WOMAN, she forgave me. Asa has been a wonderful mother and has paid for most of Logan's education. She is a wonderful human being. Thank you, Asa, for all that you have done for Logan and for all those years of putting up with me.

I also had a few talks with Logan and asked for his forgiveness as well. We now enjoy a very close relationship, and he gives me great joy. He also teaches me a lot. If I may share a Christmas card from 1994 that he recently wrote to me, it reads:

> To my Best Buddy,
>
> Thanks for being there over the years. I cherish our relationship and love you dearly. It's great to have a father who is also proud of his son, who is also proud of his boy, who gives me the confidence I need.
> Thanks for all of your love and support. I love you very much.
>
> Your boy,
> Logan

He's written me several letters like this over the years, and I have his forgiveness. We're very close and it's a great feeling. It's an honor and privilege to be a father, especially to a great son like Logan.

Lastly, I have learned to forgive myself for my past actions. I had to learn to forget my days of hustling, with the terrible guilt that plagued me for so long. I came to accept the fact that I did this not for money, though I certainly thought I was doing it for that reason at the time. In retrospect, I know it was because I had never known the love of a man. I so desperately wanted the love my father never showed me. I have no memory of him so much as hugging or kissing me.

There was one occasion when he took me to a baseball game, but that was it. He never took me to lunch at a restaurant, played catch with me, or any of those other father-and-son routines that are normal for a child. I think that is why I started to hustle.

Today I'm able to accept love from another man, but it took me a long time because I didn't trust my father. I know now that

I can hug another man, and it doesn't have to be anything sexual. This by itself represented one of the greater healing wounds in my life.

I also harbored for a long time the guilt of not going to my mother's funeral and letting my sister deal with all the myriad details. Jo-Ann forgave me, but I still had to say good-bye to my mother. I applied the Gestalt method and wrote my mother a letter telling her how wonderful she was in raising three kids without a man to help her financially. As with my father, I cried and let out the pain I had been carrying inside for years. I feel in my heart that she has forgiven me and most importantly, I have forgiven myself.

It's all been a slow process of growing up and being a responsible adult, which in all honesty, I don't want to be. I want to run for the hills like little Eddie Breitenberger and live on a mountaintop and forever avoid reality.

If I am to stay sober, it is my business to clean up my side of the street with amends, which I've done and do on a daily basis. If I am wrong, then I promptly admit it and make amends. I don't go to sleep wondering if I've offended someone. I'll call that person and tell them, "Hey look, what I said earlier today was out of line. I want to apologize. I said the wrong thing. Will you forgive me?" It's not important what they say to me or how they behave. That is none of my business. They don't even have to forgive me. My side of the street has to be constantly clean and swept. That's what keeps me from drinking. That's what keeps me sober.

It took about ninety days for the desire for alcohol to wane, but it took five years of sobriety for me to finally be at peace with myself. Every night for the first five years I *had* to be with someone. I was not comfortable to spend an evening on my own, just relaxing, reading a book, watching a movie on television, or enjoying a quiet evening by myself.

Once I reached that stage, then I learned that I could start being of service to other alcoholics, which, in all honesty, is another part of recovery. It was five years of taking on my part, and now it was time to give back. I began talking to newcomer alcoholics, sharing of my experience, strength, and hope—never giving advice, just offering my support.

For the first five years of my sobriety, I took, took, and took. That's not all bad, either. I was willing to do anything not to drink, and if by taking from the program was what kept me sober, so be it. Finally, I started to realize that I could give back. I thought, *How can I give back to the program?*

At first, I didn't have much to offer, so I offered my labor. After every meeting, I'd put away chairs and wash ashtrays and coffee cups. Then I was asked to tell my story to others in meetings. I didn't want to at first. I was totally content to listen to other speakers for the rest of my life.

"Eddie, if you're asked to speak, you speak," I was sternly told. "We don't care about your ego. We don't care about your pride. We don't care if you want to look good all the time. Just get up and speak." What I learned that day was that if someone in the program asks you to do something, you do it. I had to learn to give back what was so freely given to me. I've had men talk to me for hours on end, spoon-feeding me the program a little bit at a time.

I then graduated to sponsoring others in the program. I've actually sponsored two men, and both were perfect illustrations of how to work the program and how *not* to work the program.

The first gentleman I sponsored is a person I still sponsor today. He calls me about twice a week, and we have lunch once every three weeks. He has nine years of sobriety. He's a successful businessman who lives in Orange County with a beautiful wife and a couple of kids. We work the program and are serious about *not drinking.*

As a sponsor, I'm not very strict. I'm not a hard-liner. In fact, I inject a lot of humor in our relationship, but there are times when things get tough. Sometimes my friend will start moaning and groaning, and I tell him what a wonderful life he has. "You've got everything a man should want," I tell him. I don't try to fix him. We just talk things out, and we stay sober one day at a time.

The other gentleman who wanted me to sponsor him doesn't take his sobriety as seriously, and it shows in his life. He'd ask me for my help but would never take my suggestions. "What's the point of even talking," I'd ask him "if you don't want to listen?"

I see him every now and then, and am very courteous and polite.

"Hi, are you still going to meetings?" I ask. He might mumble, but he's obviously doing things his own way and getting nowhere in his sobriety.

The specific problem with the second guy I sponsored was that he got successful and things were going well again. He had seven years of sobriety, he got the family together, is making good money, so everything's cool. Things got too good. That's how alcoholism is—cunning, baffling, powerful, and patient—so patient, in fact, that it's waiting for the alcoholic on the sidelines doing one-armed push-ups.

I don't ever want to get to a place where I might say to myself, *Edd, you don't have to go to meetings anymore. You've got this thing licked. You don't have to share of yourself or talk with newcomers* because I know that this disease is waiting for me. If I drink again, I'm a dead man. Just because I've got a little sobriety now doesn't mean I can rest on my laurels. I keep doing what I think I should be doing, which is going to meetings and giving of myself in any way I can to others. When I'm not thinking about Edd and I'm thinking about the newcomer, I feel a whole lot better.

* * * * *

A few years ago, I had the opportunity to visit Ireland, my ancestral land. I had lived in London for so long but never had the time or opportunity to see Ireland. I was too busy drinking.

I attend a luncheon several times a week with a group of men that are recovering alcoholics. At this group, we usually share what is going on with our lives. This one fellow, Sean, shared that he was going to Ireland at the end of the week and was terribly excited.

After the luncheon, I went up and started talking to him. All of a sudden, he got me excited about the trip, and on the spur of the moment, I asked him, "Do you want some company?"

He looked at me strangely and asked, "Do you want to go?"

"Yes! I've never been there."

When this gentleman got home, he called his travel agent and made all the travel arrangements for me. We flew to London, changed planes, and flew to Dublin. We stayed in Dublin a few days and then drove to Killarney where there was a 12-step convention going on. After the convention, my friend had to go back to the States, but I decided to stay an extra two weeks. I drove to Shannon.

The first day in Shannon, I went to a well-known restaurant, and there were a lot of people milling around. I spotted this little old man who must have been around eighty years old, and I started talking to him. After a few minutes of polite conversation, I asked, "I'm going inside to have lunch, would you like to join me?" I found out he was from Canada, but was born in Ireland. He came to Ireland every year to visit while he left his wife in Toronto to do her own thing. He said, "I can't join you right now, but maybe I'll join you for a drink later on."

I went inside and ordered a salmon steak and mineral water. The eighty-year-old man came sauntering in and sat down next to me.

"What'll ya have?" I asked him.

"I'll have a Coca-Cola."

I looked at him suspiciously because he looked like an alcoholic. "Don't you drink?" I asked.

"No, not anymore. I used to."

"Oh, are you a friend of Bill's?"

Surprised, he said, "Yes, I am."

"How long have you been sober?" I continued to probe.

With an air of self-deprecating humility, he smiled and said, "Just today."

I smiled back and pressed him for an answer, "C'mon, old-timer, how long have you *really* been sober?"

"I've been sober for thirty-five years," he said proudly.

Amazed, I congratulated him, "Thirty-five years without a drink! That's quite an accomplishment."

"No, son," he corrected me, *"that's a miracle!"*

It was also on that trip to Shannon that I got to visit a castle. The beauty of the place mesmerized me. It was situated on a knoll and had a splendid view of the valley and beautiful gardens. I wandered around this castle, feeling that I had not only been there before, but somehow belonged to it.

That next morning, I awoke early and just couldn't get this castle out of my mind. I got out of bed at seven and drove over to it. No one was around. The sun was just coming up, and I was walking around the place, when I went up to the door and opened it. I went inside and again, I got that strange feeling of déjà vu that this was *my* castle and that *I* was the humble servant.

I wandered in and sat on this big bed and later wandered out into the gardens. For that full hour, I really got in touch with who I am.

There was a peace and serenity to the place as there was inside me. It was the first time that I had ever felt at peace with myself. For the first time, I had finally discovered who I really am.

* * * * *

On Friday, March 11, 1994, the Museum of Television and Radio's Eleventh Annual Festival paid tribute to *77 Sunset Strip*, as one of television's most celebrated shows.

Efrem Zimbalist, Jr., Byron Keith, who played Lieutenant Gilmore, creator and producer Roy Huggins, producers William T. Orr and Hugh Benson, director Richard L. Bare, and I were all in attendance while they screened the episode "Once Upon A Caper." This episode had all the cast members, each telling different versions of how the detective firm was founded. Roger Smith, sadly, was not able to attend.

The night was magical. After the question-and-answer session was over, in a repeat of when *Girl on the Run* first premiered in Huntington Beach, Efrem and I were again mobbed for autographs. This time, however, I was ready to deal with it.

I have finally come to terms with the fact that I will probably not come up with a character as popular as Kookie. Vince Fontaine from *Grease* gave it a good shot, but I still get more fan mail today regarding *77 Sunset Strip*.

In a melancholy mood one day, I was feeling sorry for myself and spouting off the top of my head, "What have I done in my career? I was in a couple of movies and a hit television series. Big deal! I don't really think I've accomplished that much as an actor."

My son, Logan, ever the logical one of us two, said, "Dad how many people do you know can say they were a teen idol? How many people do you know can say they had a successful television show? How many people received all of those hundreds of thousands of letters and graced the covers of magazines worldwide?"

Maybe I should do what I once told Kirk Douglas to do years ago: give myself a pat on the back.

I am grateful for everything that has happened to me. It wasn't always that way. It was like my higher power said, "OK Eddie, you want to be famous? You want to be a television star? You wanna be in the movies? You want all the luxurious homes and foreign cars?

Beautiful wife? Swimming pool? All right, Mr. Edd Byrnes, I'm going to give it to you."

At the age of twenty-five, my higher power granted me my wish, but after I got it all, this same higher power told me, "Edd, you don't seem very grateful for all that I have given you. Every fantasy, everything you've always wanted, everything you've ever dreamed of, I've given to you and you don't seem too grateful for it and are not very appreciative, so I think you need to grow up. I think I'm going to *slowly* take it all away from you."

My higher power started my "re-education" with my marriage, then the house, then the material things, and much more pain than I could ever imagine. All of this, I believe, was taken away from me, so I could be right here today in this other life, this life of sobriety. I truly believe it all had to be removed and taken away so that I could tell you my story.

Sometimes I drive by that beautiful home on Hutton Drive in Beverly Hills and the alcoholic in me says, "Eddie, boy, you really blew it. You had it all and now you have nothing." Then the sober Edd says, "I will not regret the past, and I don't dwell on it. Focus on the present, stay in the now, be grateful for what you have." And I am very grateful.

There's already a plan in my life, a mosaic, and all the pieces haven't fitted in yet. I don't know what the overall plan is and I don't have to, but I accept what is happening in my life today and I know that I am not in charge. I always thought I was in the driver's seat, but I now know that God is in charge. In fact, I am an expression of God. I feel one with my higher power.

That does not mean I can sleep all day and expect my bills to be paid. I still have to suit up and show up. I have to keep showing up and earning and not running away up into those hills thinking that I'm going to be taken care of. I think all the tragedy and pain that I went through could have been much worse, and I'm thankful to God that I'm still alive to tell you my story—so far.

The reason for all of this turmoil was to humble me. I had to discover some serenity within myself, for this day, and learn to love myself, Edd Byrnes. To take care of that frightened little kid inside of me, Eddie Breitenberger. To tell him that I love him and that I'll never leave him.

I'm glad I've had the life that I've had. It opened the door to so many things. There's no way in the world I could have met the people and experienced the things that I have if it weren't for my life as an actor. How else could I have lived in London and Rome or work in Germany, Philippines, Canada, Yugoslavia, Spain, or Italy? Or stay at the Ritz Hotel in Paris and Boston, the Plaza Hotel in New York or have tea with King Hussein of Jordan? Meet Richard Nixon, Lawrence Olivier, Rosemary Clooney, Mel Torme, Elizabeth Taylor, Richard Burton, or get to know my three godfathers. How could all these things have happened if it weren't for a loving, higher power? I am grateful now for all these memories.

There are two important things I've learned from my higher power in the past few years. First, I am *Kookie No More,* just Edd. I'm a working stiff, a normal guy, and acting just happens to be my profession. I'm a middle-income American, working and doing some traveling. Some people have a better living than I do, and a lot of people have a lot less. About 92 percent of all of the actors in the Screen Actors Guild make no more than five thousand dollars a year, so I am a very blessed person. Acting is no longer my whole life. I like it and I enjoy it. However, I must always remember that it's just something that I do for a living.

Lastly, I've learned that my higher power, God, will never leave me, that He'll always be with me. I was the one who left *Him.* He never left me.

CHAPTER EIGHTEEN

Today Is the Best Day of My Life

MY PERSONAL LIFE is calm today. I spend quality time with my son, Logan, who is a successful lawyer, but he has that adventurous streak like me. For all of the heartache I put him through, he has grown up normal and enjoys a well-adjusted life. A lot of the things in this book, he will learn about for the first time and know that his father is not perfect and that's OK. I know Logan will understand because we love each other and nothing can ever separate us.

Both Asa and I remain unmarried. I will always love her for never giving up on me when I hit my bottom. It was she who got me to that 12-step meeting where I admitted that I was powerless over alcohol and that my life was unmanageable.

Asa seems happy today. She has always been a dedicated mother to Logan and was the anchor in our family for many, many years. Coincidentally, out of all of the places to live in the West Los Angeles area, she chose to move right across the street from me, but it's a very big street!

Ironically, I think the one thing that I'm missing most in my life today is a passionate, happy, joyous, healthy relationship with a woman.

In my 12-step program, I was taught not to do anything drastic within the first year of sobriety. The suggestions are simple:114 don't change jobs; don't leave town; don't get a divorce; and don't get involved. The reason for this is really very simple and forthright. Twelve-step programs are a formula for happy and free living. After just a year, someone in recovery like me becomes a very different person. I'm not involved with anyone today, so I'm keeping myself open and vulnerable.

I don't know if I want any more children, unless a woman brought a child into the relationship. For now, I'm having fun living my own life. I travel, I go to meetings all over the world, and I appear at various collector's shows signing autographs and reminiscing with fans, which I especially enjoy. I love their enthusiasm. I guess I was part of their lives in a small way, and if I can come to their town and put a smile on their faces, it's all been worth it.

My career has even picked up again. I've been in a couple of movies the past few years, almost playing myself in nostalgic parts. In 1987, I played a parking lot attendant in *Back to the Beach.* In *Troop Beverly Hills* (1989), I costarred with Shelley Long where I played an out-of-work actor. Now that's typecasting! I played myself in an episode of *Married with Children*, one of its most popular episodes ever. In December of 1994, Logan and I flew to Munich to appear on the television show, *This Is Your Life.*

One of the things I'm proudest of is a twenty-minute short film about a man going into a bar and meeting his girlfriend. He talks to her, has a drink, then calls his wife at home. He's lying to her, saying that he's working late, and immediately after getting off the phone, he goes into the bathroom and does a line of cocaine, then comes out to talk to his girlfriend. She leaves, and he drinks some more, and slowly his progression leads him to get drunk, stoned, and feeling shame, guilt, and remorse. He then looks at himself in the mirror next to the bar and wonders, *What's going on with me?*

The final scene has him getting into his car and driving off. The audience hears this gigantic screech followed by the concussion of one big crash.

The film is shown at the Betty Ford Center in Rancho Mirage and other recuperative facilities across the country. After the film is screened, I go out and talk to the patients and tell them, "That was me up there on the screen for real." I then proceed to tell them my story.

The final purpose of this, my life's story, is not the despair and loss I've known, but rather one of hope and encouragement. For if I could overcome the tragedies and desperation in my life, I know that others whose problems may be less or worse than mine may take hope for having read these pages.

If I can get sober and *stay* sober, *anyone* can. Being powerless over alcohol is no big deal. I'm free from its grasp, and I'm grateful. I'm not lost anymore, but found. I've gotten so many rewards from going to 12-step meetings and have developed so many friendships with people who really care about me.

Today, I can handle all problems that arise. I trust my intuition and realize that God doesn't give me anything I can't handle.

Like the old-timer I shared a soda with in Ireland, I too believe in miracles. They have happened to me and countless others to whom I'm indebted for their comforting words, open minds, and giving hearts.

Miracles do happen; they happen every day.

RECOMMENDED READING

THESE ARE JUST but a few books I recommend to read. They have helped throughout the years to keep me sober. They are:

24 Hours A Day, published by Hazelden

Daily Reflections, published by Alcoholics Anonymous World Service, Inc.

Daily Affirmations For Adult Children Of Alcoholics by Rokelle Lerner, published by Health Communications.

Alcoholics Anonymous published by World Service, Inc.

Twelve Steps and Twelve Traditions published by Alcoholics Anonymous World Service, Inc.

How To Get Out Of Debt, Stay Out Of Debt And Live Prosperously by Jerrold Mundis

Atlas Shrugged by Ayn Rand (an excellent money book for women)

The Dynamic Laws Of Prosperity by Catherine Ponder

Money Is My Friend by Phil Laut published by Trinity Publications

INDEX